Speak Easy

The Survival Guide
to Speech and Public Speaking

Second Edition

Ruth,
With fondness + appreciation! Looking
forward to a wonderful friendship.
Blessings,
Mark
August 2009

R. Mark Giuliano, D.Min.

WILLIAMS & COMPANY
BOOKPUBLISHERS

ISBN 1-878853-85-6

Printed in the United States of America

For Beth, Dylan and Daryl

A word fitly spoken is like apples of gold
in a setting of silver.

Proverbs 25:11

Acknowlededements

MANY THANKS TO ALL those who have encouraged me to teach and to write, especially Roger Ross, Carolyn Babcock and all my esteemed colleagues in the School of Liberal Arts at The Savannah College of Art and Design, Gail Eubanks at Savannah Technical College, Tom Hines at Savannah State University, Keith Craig, Julie Stone, Tom and Christina Williams, my mother, Betty Giuliano, and the wonderfully imaginative and supportive people of Montgomery Presbyterian Church.

Table of Contents

Part One

Getting Started

—1—

Taking the Leap

Mastering the art and craft of public speaking is a lot like learning to jump off the high diving board. At first it takes more courage than you think you could ever muster. But once you take that first successful plunge you quickly discover within yourself a well of untapped confidence!

WHEN I WAS A BOY, one of my greatest fears was jumping off the high diving board into the sixteen foot deep-end of our neighborhood public swimming pool. Just the thought of climbing up all those wet and slippery steps while lifeguards and other swimmers watched made me weak in the knees. What if I slipped on the way up? I'm pretty sure I had seen that before—or maybe it was just in my imagination. What if I froze at the top and had to inch my way back down those wet and slippery steps in embarrassment? My friends and especially my two older brothers would never let me forget it.

I remember the day I made my first leap. It was during swimming lessons. I was five or six years old. I had been given a red wristband that said I was a strong enough swimmer to swim in the deep end. What were they thinking! So what if I could tread water for five minutes. In my mind, I knew that I was far better at the 'dead-man's float' and I really didn't want to be forced to use it now. But my teacher, a confident young teenager for whom I had a great deal of respect, told the class that she would climb up the ladder with us. She would be right behind us and when we got onto the diving board, she would be there to walk us through the basics, every step of the way. And that she did.

That day, with the help of my teacher, I was able to master jumping off the high-diving board. Oh, I probably looked a little like a cat being thrown into the pool at first, arms flailing, water streaming up my nose at contact, but by the end of the first class, I was jumping a pretty darn good jump. After a while, I was even doing it without the help of my teacher. Proud of myself I thought, "Gee, if I can do this, I will be able to do just about anything. Maybe astronaut isn't entirely out of the question after all!"

As you can imagine, I was eager to race home and tell my family about my accomplishments but on the way home I fell off my bike and smashed my baby toe. But that's another story.

It was later in the week (once my toe nail had fallen off completely) that I risked an actual dive. And later in the summer when my brothers and I rode our bikes down to the pool for open swim, I proudly displayed some of my more complex moves: cannon ball, jack knife and the crowd stopping, "guy reading newspaper."

As I look back on it, mastering the art and craft of public speaking is a lot like learning to jump off the high diving board. At first it takes more courage than you think you could ever muster. But once you take that first successful plunge you quickly discover within yourself a well of untapped confidence.

Indeed, there is a big leap of faith required—at least the first time or two, but with the aid of our teachers and guide books, such as the one you are reading now, a little time and experience, you quickly develop the basics and learn how to maneuver those slippery steps so that you can get up in front of an audience in spite of any remnant weak-kneed jitters. In time, you may even discover that you actually enjoy yourself while you're doing it.

With a small amount of effort and a willingness to take

the leap into the world of public speaking, you will develop an authentic confidence that will spill over into many other places in your life, as well. And whether you are doing an oral cannonball or rhetorical jack-knife, you most certainly won't be doing any public speaking belly flops—unless, of course, that is your intention. But, hey, you'll probably be able to do it without getting any words up your nose.

— 2 —

Opening the Doors of Opportunity: Learning to Speak Easy

IN 1919, THE UNITED STATES congress passed an anti-alcohol law called the National Prohibition Act of 1919 (sometimes referred to as the Volstead Act named, aptly, after Minnesota Congressman, Andrew Volstead, who introduced it). One of the outcomes of making alcohol illegal, except in certain circumstances, was the grass roots development of the "speakeasy." The speakeasy was a saloon where alcohol was sold illegally. Some historians suggest the term 'speakeasy' reflected the way one was to speak about and within the illegal tavern. A word quietly spoken would allow for the survival of the saloon.

The word "speakeasy" is also suggestive of the way one gained access to the bar—by softly speaking a password, which would open the door. If one didn't know a particular speakeasy's code word, access likely would not be granted. It was knowing the right word and where and when to speak it, which opened the door to the forbidden drink. Good oral communication has always been about speaking the right word, opening doors and gaining access to rooms of new thought, opportunity and advancement.

Communication: The Key to Your Success

Say it loud and say it proud! Or at least say it well and say it with confidence. After all, effective communication is the key to your success!

Every quarter, four quarters a year, by choice, my colleagues and I undertake one of the greatest challenges life has to offer: teaching mandatory public speaking classes in the largest art and design school in America, the Savannah College of Art and Design (SCAD). Now, if you are like any of the one thousand or so young people who, each year, muster up their courage and drag themselves, kicking and screaming, into a required Speech 105 class, you might be wondering why speech and public speaking is so important anyway. I know most my students wonder why! After all, these students are studying to be everything from architects and painters to graphic designers and sequential artists, from photographers and fashion designers to filmmakers and product designers. Why on earth should they bother with such seemingly trivial matters as speech and public speaking?

In fact, this is the precise question I ask each introductory speech class to consider: Why would an art and design school make public speaking a required course? Actually, I first ask them how many would take the class if it were not required. Usually one or two respond favorably. Most sort of giggle sheepishly as if their secret has been found out. For most of my students, speech class is a chore, a hoop through which every one has to jump or, as one student so honestly put it, "a necessary evil."

But am I discouraged? Never! Teaching public speaking is not for the faint of heart! Besides, after a brief discussion, inevitably my bright young students are able to offer me some sound and positive responses that point to the value of oral communication in every chosen profession.

An architect in training will tell me that if she is going convince a prospective client, not only will she need to use computer generated images and small-scale 3-D models, but she will have to use her words. A fashion designer will agree and remind the class that the spoken word is an essential tool both for interpersonal communication and, professionally, for selling ideas.

Getting the Job

I wait for an opportune time and chime in with a little but important fact that I copped from Osborn and Osborn's excellent text book, *Public Speaking* 5th Edition. In 1996, the National Association of Colleges and Employers surveyed hundreds of corporate head hunters to discern desirable characteristics in potential recruits, that is to say, the kinds of things employers are looking for in prospective employees. The results were astonishing. Of the eleven characteristics or skills identified, effective oral communication was deemed the most important. That means, all else being equal (grades, schools, etc.), the person with the best communication skills will likely get the job! Often times employers will even hire a candidate with a lower GPA or less work experience than other hopefuls if that candidate can communicate well. In other words, good communication skills give you the edge in landing the job of your choice.

But good oral communication can produce even sweeter fruits than just "getting the job."

> All else being equal, the person with the best communication skills will likely get the job!

Confidence

At the end of a quarter, students often tell me that they feel like they can accomplish so much more now that they have mastered their anxiety and developed both the practical skills and the personal courage to stand up in front of a group of people and give a talk. One student confided that he wished he hadn't put-off his speech class for so long. It was eating away at him all through college. But now that he had confronted his fear, taken the class and done well with it, it had a spill-over effect in other areas of his academics and his life in general. He felt better about himself. He boasted with a well-earned, self-congratulating chuckle, "If I can handle speech class, I can handle just about anything!"

I bumped into a former student at the store one day who told me that he had been paying his way through college working as a guide for a Savannah-based company that offered historical walking tours with a ghost theme. He said that his public speaking tools had helped him gain more confidence for keeping clients entertained and interested.

In a way, developing yourself as a speaker will have confidence building effects similar to those gained by working-out. The stronger we feel about ourselves in one area of our lives (one of the scariest!), the more confidence we feel in other areas. There is an amazing sense of personal strength and discovery we gain when not only do we know what we want to say and how to say it, but that we can say it in front of a group of people, large or small—and nobody laughs or misunderstands us. Once we discover that we can over come one of the most common fears among all human beings, then we will feel like we have an edge over most other things too.

Of course, there are lots of other benefits you will receive by learning to speak well and speak easy. Developing an ability to articulate your feelings and ideas in a group setting will augment your ability to speak confidently and concisely in interpersonal relationships, as well. For example, your 'significant other' will thank you and love you all the more for becoming an articulate communicator. After all, how many times have we found ourselves stumbling around in the dark searching for the right words to express our feelings to someone special or nervously tripping over our own tongues even when we knew precisely what we wanted to say.

As we develop good speech communication skills we have the opportunity to strengthen our interpersonal communication skills, as well.

Do actions speak louder than words?
We have all heard the saying: actions speak louder than words. If actions do, in fact, speak louder than words, maybe the question shouldn't be, "Why do we have to take speech class?" Rather, "Why should we speak at all?" If our actions speak louder than words, maybe we should just stick to classes in architecture

> There is an amazing sense of personal strength and discovery we gain when not only do we know what we want to say and how to say it, but that we can say it in front of a group of people, large or small.

or film studies, or the fine arts such as painting or sculpture. Who needs words when you have a perfectly good action?

Speaking Clarifies Action

If we think about it for a moment, we soon realize that so many of the things we do need words to explain why we did them. Slamming down the telephone on your girlfriend or boyfriend may be an action clearly expressing your anger but ten minutes later you may need to call back and use your words to talk about why you were angry. You need your words to clarify the action. Marching up and down Main Street because you want your government to make a commitment to peace has a far greater effect if you paint words on placards and protest signs, or shout out the slogans of peace in chants or speeches. Our actions need words to give them strength and clarity. Our words define the action.

Our actions need words to give them strength and clarity. Our words define and clarify the action.

Similarly, an architect may have designed a wonderful model of a proposed plan, but the plan will need some explanation to help clients understand the benefits of adopting the plan. In fact, a good architect will begin a relationship with a potential client simply by listening. The first step is hearing the client's vision, helping the client to use his or her words to articulate that vision. Models and drawings come much later. Or a painter who is commissioned by a city to paint a mural on a local community center may need to use words to explain the proposal in advance of the commission. Sometimes words are necessary to clarify action.

Speaking Can Be More Efficient Than Action

There are many instances in our lives where actions can be too unwieldy and only words will help us get our point across. Have you ever tried to order a sandwich in a local café without words? Of course, you could sketch your order or model it in clay, but if you have only 30 minutes to order and eat, words will be far more helpful. Words, whether spoken, written, typed or entered, are still the primary vehicle of communication throughout our rapidly changing world. They are still the most efficient means of expressing ideas, needs, wants and desires. Admittedly, there are times efficiency is not the issue, but for the most part, if we want to get along in the world on a daily basis, more often than not, we will use words.

Speaking Brings Meaning to Action

Action is good. But sometimes when actions are accompanied with words, the action takes on deeper meaning. Once a month in my church, as the pastor, I do something that might be meaningless to some people without words. I lift a loaf of bread in the air and show it to everyone. Then I break it in two. Afterwards, I pour grape juice into a goblet and lift it up for everyone in the room to see. A strange action, indeed. If you have never participated in this action, the Sacrament of Holy Communion or The Lord's Supper, you would have no idea of what was happening unless you heard the accompanying words which tell the story of how the night before Jesus was arrested he took some bread and broke it in two, saying, "this is my body broken for you" and then poured some wine into a cup and said, "this is my blood poured out for the forgiveness of sins."

Without the words, the meaning of the action is missed or soon forgotten. I recall a number of years ago, my wife and I had taken our children to worship in a neighborhood church one Christmas Eve. The minister invited us to come forward to receive communion. When we came back to our seats, my six year old son had obviously missed the words of consecration—the retelling of the story, and asked, "Hey, did you guys get some juice boxes up there?" Often, actions without words are confusing at best.

More Than Words

But sometimes, it is more than words which bring meaning to our actions; it is the human voice with its personal rhythm, syntax and cadence which brings deeper meaning to our actions. It is the human voice that resonates the vibration of the heart with clarity and immediacy.

Like most kids who grew up in Canada during the 1970s, one of my greatest memories was seeing Paul Henderson of Team

Canada score in overtime during game eight to help Canada beat the Soviet Union in international hockey. It was the first time a western, democratic nation had played an eastern, communist nation. It was in the midst of the bitterly Cold War. To most Canadians Henderson's goal was 'the shot that could be heard around the world.' As the Canadian rock group, The Tragically Hip, put it back in the 1990s: "If there was a goal that everyone remembers, it was back in old '72." That was Henderson's goal. Most Canadians worth their weight in snow will remember that particular goal above most others. What a sweet memory.

But in my mind, Henderson's goal is accompanied by an announcer's voice screaming four words at the top of his lungs with uncontrolled and unabashed exhilaration: "Henderson, Henderson! He scores!" It was the announcer's voice and his words that heightened the excitement of that goal for me. The event, the words, the voice, they all gel together to express deep and lasting meaning for me and millions of other proud Canadians.

Maya Angelou once said that our "words mean more that what is set down on paper. It takes the human voice to infuse them with shades of deeper meaning." Just imagine the difference between silently reading the words of Rev. Dr. Martin Luther King's *I Have a Dream* speech compared to hearing them rise up with passion and conviction. True, the words on their own have a certain power, but once spoken aloud they are truly infused with deeper meaning.

Speaking is Action

One of the most common, yet subtle, misunderstandings we share in the western world about the spoken word is that speaking is passive, whereas, our actions are, well, active. When we think of doing, we rarely think of words or speaking. Many students are eager to hurdle public speaking and get on to the good stuff—the active classes such as, drawing, sculpting, computer animation, etc.—the "doing" classes. But speaking itself is an action.

Speaking is a performance piece in a sense. At a very base level, our body is actively producing a sound. Blood is pumping more oxygen to the brain and to our muscles. Hopefully, we are taking some deeper breaths to supply more oxygen to our cardiovascular system. Our diaphragm releases and tightens pushing air upwards and vibrating across the vocal chords. Sound is produced. Our tongues regulate the sound. Filter it. Slur it. Make it hiss or whistle like steam escaping from a kettle. Sometimes our tongues sound a "tick-tock" like a clock. Our mouths shape the sound. Smooth it or round it out. Bump it with our lips. Perhaps our bodies are getting in on the action too, animating what we are saying with a waving arm or a tightened fist. This is action.

But action is occurring at another level too. When we speak publicly, people gather; minds, ideas, experiences and agendas are shaped by our words.

When MLK spoke on the steps of the Lincoln Memorial thousands of people were brought together. In many ways, it was his words that called those people to travel many miles from across the nation and gather as one in protest against violations to human rights. It was his words that shaped both the agenda of the Civil Rights movement and the actions of those who were involved in it. His words both reflected and infused meaning and truth that still stand today. MLK's famous speech painted the picture, which would become the vision for the entire movement. His words inspired and motivated people in the moment. It gave them strength and courage to face the injustices which they encountered in their day-to-day battles against localized racism and systemic bigotry.

> "The most political statement we can make today is to say, 'I love you.'"
> —Sting

Perhaps the nineteenth century German philosopher, Friedrich Hegel said it best: "Our speeches are actions among people, and indeed, most effective ones."

There is an ancient Hebrew word, *dabar*, which means "word-event." There was an understanding among the ancients that speaking not only created an event but also *was* an event—something that could never be entirely recreated because, even though the words might be the same, the gathering, the context, the time, the people, the emotions and feelings of the moment all would be different.

Have you ever gone to hear someone speak and tape-record-ed the speech. When you got home all excited to play the tape for some one else, it didn't seem to be the same. You may have end-ed up letting out a disappointed sigh and saying something like, "Well, I guess you had to be there." And that would be the most accurate thing you could say. The speech was more than passive words floating around in an undefined space. The speech was an action, deeply connected to, and in part, responsible for the event.

> **When we speak publically, people gather—and minds, ideas, exeriences and agendas are shaped by our words.**

Our words are hardly passive. In fact, they become danger-ous tools if we do not understand the power our words do have. Do you remember the big lie we all learned as children: sticks and stones may break my bones, but names will never hurt me? Perhaps children, more than anyone, know that that little verse is agonizingly inaccurate. Fatso, four eyes, string bean, pork chop, carrot top, buck-toothed-bucky, tinsel teeth. These are just a few of the hurtful names that kids can sling at one another—simple words which can be more strikingly painful and long lasting than even the most jagged of stones.

On the other hand, there are amazing and positive outcomes when we use our words creatively for good. And when we do, we gain a tremendous sense of self-fulfillment and personal sat-isfaction. Shortly after the September 11, 2001 terrorist attacks on the United States, the British rock musician, Sting, said on Good Morning America that the most political statement we can make today consists of three words: "I love you."

Our words can be used in many helpful ways: to build-up others, offer hope, or even teach. Whether it is offering directions to a tourist or extending words of encouragement to a grieving group of people at a funeral, our words have an awesome pow-er to shape the lives of others. And when we use them in helpful ways, those same words have a power to make us feel great!

Human speech is critical. As infants, from the time we could squawk, we were attempting to communicate. We communicate interpersonally and in groups for a variety of reasons: to express needs and wants, to articulate our feelings, to be understood and to understand others, to teach and to learn.

It doesn't matter what your profession is, or who you are, oral communication is necessary. And the better you are at it, the happier and more successful you will be and the greater the contribution you will make to the world around you and the people within it.

Upon Reflection

1. What actions do you do which need words to clarify or explain?
2. What words or names have had a power, which you could feel emotionally or even physically?
3. What words have come to life for you recently simply by having heard them spoken aloud?
4. Read a favorite poem in your head. Read the same poem, aloud. Does it take on a different meaning when spoken aloud?

— 3 —

The Fear Factor:
Loosening Anxiety's Grip

"I've gone hang-gliding. I've gone skydiving. I like things that are a little scary. Maybe that's why I do [stand-up comedy]. I read a thing that actually speaking in front of a crowd is considered the number one fear of the average person. I found that amazing. Number two was death! Number two. That means to the average person that if you have to be at a funeral you would rather be in the casket than doing the eulogy."
– Jerry Seinfeld, from *I'm Telling You for the Last Time*

WHAT SCARES YOU? HEIGHTS? Closed spaces? Death? Or is it dying? Woody Allen once joked, "I'm not afraid to die. I just don't want to be there when it happens!" If you are like most Americans, you probably have some inhibitions about speaking in public. In study after study, the fear of speaking in front of a group of people, large or small, ranks as one of the most common and worst of all our fears. For some, the thought speaking in front of a group of people is even more frightening than death. And like Woody Allen, we'd rather not be there when it happens! That's why Jerry Seinfeld once pointed out that according to statistics, if we were at a funeral, we would rather be the one being eulogized and than the one delivering the eulogy!

And Now for a Story: We All Have Our Moments!
I remember all too vividly the first time I had to give a speech, although I wish I didn't. Actually, "sermon" would be a better term than "speech," though. After all, it was in a church. But whatever the term, it was still a disaster and I was left wishing I had taken

a public speaking course before hand or, at the very least, a class to help me deal with my dormant anxiety about speaking in public which decided to reveal itself in an untimely manner just hours before my first big speaking gig.

I was a graduate student of theology at McGill University in Montréal. I had been invited to go speak at a little country church on the occasion of Theological Education Sunday—that special Sunday when universities and seminaries send out students to speak to congregations about coughing-up a little more green to help prepare men and women for vocations in ministry.

Why on earth they sent out students to do the job, I'll never know. Sure we seminarians were eager and thought we had a lot, if not all, of the answers to people's burning questions about God and the sorry state of the world. But if the truth be known, at least in my case, I humbly confess, seminary students who had yet to take a speaking course were the worst ones to send out to speak to congregations. Then again, maybe that was the plan: show churches just how pathetic we were and maybe they'd take pity and give more!

Getting Ready

In preparation the week before, I had pecked out a full manuscript on my new electronic typewriter—a Brother no less! And not only was I hi-tech, but medium and message were working together in symbiotic harmony. What I wrote seemed brilliantly authored, clear and meaningful. "People will laugh," I congratulated myself, "and then people will cry. But most of all, I will be amazing!" Mine were the kind of naive and unsuspecting thoughts that many novices experience: "just give me half a chance and I'll really wow them!"

A Funny Thing Happened

But the day before the big speaking engagement, when I went off to my guest room to go over my notes, an odd thing happened to me. What I had written back in the city didn't seem to make much sense out there in the country. In fact, what I had written the previous week didn't seem to make much sense, period. I began to panic. The words that I had so carefully crafted just one week earlier started jumping around on the page. I was beginning to feel a little queasy.

The morning I was to speak in that little country church, still not quite understanding that the problem wasn't with my manuscript but with my anxiety about speaking in front of an audience, I decided to make a strategic move and abandon my manuscript altogether. "I can just wing it," I reasoned. "It will probably make more sense anyway." With that, I began to calm down . . . just a bit.

The Big Moment

Well, the big moment came. The Pastor introduced me to the congregation. Kind words, I am told. But I heard none of it. All I could hear was the sound of my own heart beating wildly in my chest like a kick drum at a rock concert, my blood pumping steadily behind my ears like a runaway fright train screaming out of control. My stomach hadn't felt so bad since the time I had gorged myself on too many BB Bats, Rockets and bite-sized Kit Kat bars against my parent's stern warnings one memorable Halloween years earlier. I wasn't sweating or shaking but just seconds before standing up to speak my vision started to go blurry.

Mercifully, I suppose, I was switched on to autopilot. From the moment I faced my audience until I was standing with the minister shaking people's hands following the service, I remember absolutely nothing.

When it was all over, one very large, gruff looking man came up to greet me after my speech. He took my soft, little seminarian's hand in his beefy and calloused farmer's hand and growled, "I want to talk to you about what you said about unions!" I offered him a weak smile and choked through a dry and crackly voice, "Unions? Did I same something about unions?"

Communication Apprehension? You Are Not Alone!

If you haven't guessed it by now, I am challenged by something called *communication apprehension* or *performance anxiety*. I just shared a story with you about the first time I experienced this very real, potentially incapacitating but common problem. That was almost twenty years ago. I'd like to tell you that I don't experience performance anxiety any longer. But I can't, because I do. The good news, however, is that I can confidently tell you that I rarely *suffer* from communication apprehension anymore.

It may seem odd to you, that I, a speech and public speaking professor who preaches in a church at least once a week, would have speaking anxiety. But consider this: the fear of speaking in public is one of the most common and one of the most debilitating fears. If you are even the slightest bit nervous about speaking in public, you are not alone. Join the club!

Take Heart. There is Help!

Experiencing communication apprehension, to one degree or another, is normal. Suffering from it, however, is not necessary. In the words of M. Kathleen Casey, "Pain is inevitable. Suffering is optional."

First things first: There is a difference between experiencing stress and having an anxiety disorder. There is a difference between having some occasional anxiety, which is not only normal and, in some circumstances, helpful, and having an on going problem with anxiety. Don't let your nervousness before a speech fool you. You are going to be okay and below I will help you understand what happens to you when you are experiencing a little stage fright, why we get anxious when we have to give a speech and some tried and true tools for negotiating your way around your communication apprehension. If you think you may have a more serious problem with anxiety, I have provided a list of some helpful resources at the end of this chapter.

Stressed? Know the Signs.

Talking always helps. When people share aloud their own apprehensions about giving speeches, they are usually surprised, and, more importantly, relieved to discover that there are others who

> The fear of speaking in public is one of the most common and one of the most debilitating fears. If you are even the slightest bit nervous about speaking in public, you are not alone. Join the club!

feel exactly the same way they do. The following is a compilation of things college students from all parts of the world experience prior to or during a speech:

- Heart beats more quickly
- Forget to breathe
- Start shallow breathing
- Can't see—everything gets blurry
- Hands shake
- Rock back and forth on feet
- Face goes beet red
- Can't remember anything
- Voice quivers or shakes
- Uncontrollable sweating
- Hands get cold and clammy
- Have to go to the bathroom

Why Do We Get Anxious Before a Speech?

Underlying our fear of speaking in public is a fear of making a fool out of ourselves: saying the wrong thing, looking foolish or sounding stupid. When I graduated from Vanderbilt my mother mailed me a graduation card. On the front there was an illustration of a proud graduate wearing an ear-to-ear smile. The caption read: Son, Today you graduate. After many years of hard work and dedication, you will walk across the stage to receive your diploma. But when I opened the card, it read: Make sure your fly is done up! No matter how skilled we are, how educated we may be, we still have a nagging fear that when we get up in front of a group of people our proverbial fly may be down!

Particularly, but not exclusively, teens and young adults have a fear of being judged. But remember, everyone is in the same boat. Even speech professors and professional speakers get nervous before a speech.

At a deeper level, however, all of us understand that when we share our words in a speech, we are really sharing a part of ourselves. This creates inner conflict or anxiety. On the one hand, we

Bonus Track
When you relax an audience with humor, you will relax yourself, as well. This is creating positive audience feedback and using it to your advantage.

believe that we have something valuable, meaningful or important to say and may even be glad for an opportunity to talk about it. On the other hand, we worry that if our audience rejects our words, they will reject us.

There is a verse from an Indigo Girls song that illustrates vividly the double-edged sword of speaking: "The words of my heart are lined up like prisoners along a fence." On the one hand, we may have deep feelings about a subject - our words, like prisoners along a fence, are eager to get out. They search longingly for freedom through expression. And yet, our words can be, at the very same time, lined up along a fence like prisoners awaiting execution. Our ideas and our feelings may run the risk of being shot down by an audience.

To speak is to risk. In public speaking there is both the promise of the imagination's liberation through our well-crafted words and the threat of rejection by those who may not understand. Our anxiety is well founded!

The Dandy Dozen: 12 Remarkable Relaxation Techniques
While you may experience anxiety, you do not have to let it have its way with you. The following is a list with some things that either I have found helpful or my students have found helpful.

1. Don't Sweat Your Anxiety. Yes, I know. It sounds easier said than done. But our anxiety is both natural and normal. It is part of that fight or flight instinct that we all have. Your mind and your body are getting you ready to deal with a stressful situation. Instead of being caught off guard by your anxiety, you can welcome it and put it to work for you. Turn it to your advantage by changing some of that nervous negative energy into positive and helpful energy. It is an energy source after all. Use it to help you speak more loudly and clearly. Let that energy animate your body. Who says you have to rigidly hang on to the side of the podium. You can move about a bit. Make some appropriate facial expressions and hand gestures. All that nervous energy can help you out once you acknowledge and befriend it. Besides, more often than not, when we fight it, it makes us more nervous. So relax about being nervous and roll with it!

2. Make the Audience Feel Great about Themselves. For most of us, when we have to give a speech, our first worry is about ourselves—what we will look like or what we will sound like, etc. But if we can start thinking of the audience as our most important concern, we will invariably take the focus off ourselves. If we devote our attention to helping the audience understand our ideas or making the audience feel respected and important, we will take the attention off ourselves and put it where it belongs: on the audience. Not only will we make the audience feel great about listening to our speech, but also by getting the attention off of ourselves we will reduce our anxiety greatly. Not to mention, it builds up our own personal integrity as a speaker. (see Ethos in Chapter 4). Here are a few ways you can make people in an audience feel good about themselves:

- Thank them for allowing you the opportunity to speak;
- Compliment them on their venue or the meal they just served you (even if you were a little too nervous to enjoy it!);
- With permission, share an important comment that one of them shared with you prior to the speech;
- Tell them a humorous story or a joke. Who doesn't enjoy laughter? And besides, if you can get the audience to relax a little bit, you will relax more too! (Warning: If you are not funny, don't try to be. Honor your strengths and your weaknesses!) For more on humor, see Chapter 17.

3. Remember that No One is Perfect—Not Even You! Who said your speech has to be perfect? Only you. And who defines perfection in a speech anyway? In his book, *Getting the Word Across*, Princeton Speech Communication professor, Robert Jacks, has an excellent chapter called "There is a God and You Are Not It!" Jacks reminds us of the adage, "nobody is perfect."

4. Even if You Have An Ugly Dog—Walk It Proudly! Why not act confidently? No one except you knows just how you are feeling when you are giving a speech. How many times have we felt like we were falling apart during a speech only to hear somebody say, "You didn't seem nervous at all." Or, how many times did we feel like our speech was a real bomb and yet others said they felt like we were talking directly to them? No one hears the little crackle in the voice or feels the heavy thumping of the heart as much as we do. Besides, when we act confidently (not cocky) we relax the audience who may be anxious for us at the beginning. And, cyclically, when the audience relaxes, we relax. So, even if you feel like your speech is an ugly dog—walk it proudly!

5. Say It Don't Read It. For a variety reasons, it is always better to use an outline rather than a fully written out manuscript. First, audiences don't know what you are going to say next so even if you do get a little off track, everyone is none the wiser except you.

Secondly, when we have a full manuscript and we are even the slightest bit nervous, we are tempted to read the speech. That becomes extremely boring for the audience. Snore! And if the audience is drifting off to dreamland, it will make us even more nervous. Also, when we read, we tend to follow along each line with our finger. And then we panic if we lose our spot. If you have an outline, with key points and a rough idea of what you want to say you are rarely in danger of augmenting your anxiety because you got lost.

Thirdly, what you have to say in the moment is usually far more dynamic and far more interesting than what you had pecked out the night before in front of your computer. Writing and speaking are two very different types of communication.

6. Breathe! When we get nervous we tend to take short, shallow breaths. Our shallow breathing often makes us stutter or stammer or even rush through our sentences. Deep breathing and/or meditation can greatly reduce our anxiety and help us speak more clearly. One of the most helpful breathing techniques I have come across is one that Anthony Weil, MD wrote about in his book, *Eight Weeks to Optimum Health*. We can easily practice this remarkable relaxation technique by finding a quiet place, sitting comfortably upright with our eyes closed and then breathing in through our nose for four seconds. Once our lungs are full, we hold our breath for seven seconds. After which, we exhale with some slight resistance (tongue curled and pressed to the back of our upper teeth or through pursed lips) for eight seconds. If we repeat this exercise for four or five repetitions we will be amazed at how relaxed we feel.

7. Walk, Run or Pump Iron. One of the most effective ways of relaxing is exercising. If we have excess energy, we will need to find a way to use it to our advantage or burn it off before it becomes a problem for us. A good long walk or other exercise can be a great remedy for getting rid of nervous energy.

8. Out With the Bad, In with the Good. If you are experiencing negative thoughts, replace them with positive ones with two similar techniques called cognitive restructuring and visualization. If you are filled with thoughts and images of failure, you just may be aiding and abetting a self-fulfilling prophecy. However, if you can imagine your speech going well, chances are it will go well!

9. Talk About What You Know. Sometimes we are far more comfortable talking about familiar subjects or relating topics to things that are familiar to us. I once had a student, a part-time waitress, who talked about people's personality types by the kinds of dressing they chose for their salads. Not only was it dynamic, lively, and interesting to everybody, but she had a great time giving the speech.

10. Know About What You Talk. You will be far more relaxed if you have researched your topic thoroughly, organized it in a simple but meaningful way, and have taken the time to learn your speech well enough to deliver it without having to read it.

11. It Was Probably Something You Ate. There are certain foods, which some people find comforting. Chocolate is my archenemy. I am tempted to eat it when I am nervous. But because it is filled with caffeine and sugar, it ends up making me feel worse in the end. If you need to eat for comfort, try to stick to whole foods with low natural sugars. Avoid foods and drinks containing caffeine! There are, on the other hand, some excellent herbal products, which will greatly reduce stress and anxiety. A popular one among my students is a floral extract called *Rescue Remedy*. Check your local health food store.

12. Practice!!! Perhaps one of the most effective approaches to reducing anxiety before a speech is to be well prepared. Make sure you have done a great job writing, outlining and then, most importantly, learning your speech! The more you know what you are going to say, the more comfortable you will be saying it. Note: There is a difference between knowing your speech and memorizing your speech. Don't try to memorize your speech verbatim. Memorization simply creates more anxiety. And if you lose your spot, you will panic. On the other hand, knowing precisely what you want to say, and roughly what words you will use to say it, allows you to be comfortable with your speech - even if it doesn't come out, word for word, the way you rehearsed it.

Upon Reflection

1. Do you remember your first public speaking experience? Did you get nervous? If so, what were some of the physical or emotional responses you had to your nervousness?

2. What are some relaxation techniques you have found helpful in other stressful situations? How can they be helpful to you before or during a speech?

3. If you were at a funeral, would you rather be the one in the casket or the one giving the eulogy?

Postscript

If you suspect that you have a more serious problem with stress or anxiety, consult a health care professional. As well, here are a few excellent resources, among many, that I have found helpful:

- **Anxiety Network of Australia.** Offers education and information, treatments and remedies, and much more. http://www.anxietynetwork.com.au/
- **F. L. Holtz, Ph.D. Psychologist.** Offers lots of information, a free evaluative tool (self-examination) and tips for dealing with anxiety. http://www.therapy-now.com/index.html

- *Healing Anxiety Naturally* by Harold. Bloomfield, M.D. (New York: Harper Collins, 1998; ISBN 0-06-019127-9. Bloomfield's excellent book defines different types of anxiety, natural treatments for anxiety, stress and insomnia, as well, as self-understanding and empowerment tools for dealing with "mild to moderate" anxiety.

Part Two

The Speaker

- 4 -

Developing Your Credibility

"I'm good enough. I'm smart enough. And, gosh, people like me!"
—Stewart Smiley, *Saturday Night Live*

NOW HERE IS AN INTERESTING question: Why should any audience want to listen to us? Oh, we may think that we are entertaining or have wonderful things to say, but unless our audience already has some sort of prior relationship with us, or prior knowledge about us, there is really no reason they should be bending over backwards to hear what we have to say.

Of course, if we are already a superstar in our particular field, or are renowned for our amazing gifts as a public speaker, audiences may eagerly await our well-crafted words and edifying delivery. For most of us, however, we will need to develop some ways to encourage an audience's interest in our speech and their trust in us.

If people are going to listen to us, they will have to like us— at least a little bit! Whether we are preparing an Informative Speech, a Persuasive Speech or even a wedding toast, our personal credibility with our audience is one of the most important tools we have at our disposal.

Bonus Track
The more you ask of an audience, the more important your personal integrity is!

In the last chapter, I told you a story about my first big speaking engagement—an embarrassing fiasco in a little country church where my mind went blank and I said things of which I have no recollection. I made a lot of mistakes that day! One of the biggest was that I didn't ask myself that important personal credibility question: Why would these people want to listen to me? I naively believed that since I was a graduate student people would just naturally want to hear what I had to say.

Wow, was I mistaken! These people were gracious and welcomed me to their humble congregation, but by and large, they listened to me like you might listen to a traveling salesperson - with a great deal of suspicion. After all, I was not one of them. I was an outsider. I was from the city and they were from the country. I was young and they were older. I had a lot of book learning. They had real life training. And, as difficult as it is to admit, I was quite arrogant and they could see that in me!

Obviously, the problem wasn't them—it was me. I did nothing to confront these kinds of personal issues in my speech. I didn't give my audience very much to accept me as a credible speaker.

According to Aristotle*, the most effective speeches contain three important elements: ethos, logos and pathos. Ethos is the personal credibility or personal character of the speaker. Without it, we might as well gather up our numbered note cards and go home!

> If we want an audience to listen to us, they will need to gain a sense that we have made them our most important priority.

The great thing about developing ethos is that not only does it build up an audience's trust in you, but it also has the power to relax them, and in turn, you! Never underestimate the power of ethos.

I know what you are thinking: If I've never given a speech before or I have never given a speech to this particular audience before, how will they know how credible I am? Fear not! There are some basic tools that you can weave into your speech which will help you develop your ethos with your audience and help relax you as a speaker.

A speaker with solid credibility exhibits four important characteristics: personal integrity, friendliness, competence and dynamic presence.

Four Characteristics of a Great Speaker

1. Personal Integrity. A speaker who wants to enhance ethos will need to exhibit personal integrity. A person of integrity is concerned about the audience over and above anything else. As I mentioned in the last chapter, by putting the focus on the audience, we can reduce our own anxiety. But it is more than that. Making the audience feel respected is probably the most important thing we can do to gain people's attention and receive their respect in return.

Be Straight with Your Audience: You don't need to trick an audience to get them to listen to your ideas. I had a student who once said, "When I hear politicians speak, I really never trust what I am hearing. You never seem to get a straight answer. No wonder we think they are crooked!" If audiences are to trust us, we will need to be able to communicate in a simple, honest and straightforward manner.

Present All Sides of a Subject or Issue: Demonstrate a respect for your audience by incorporating, or at the very least, acknowledging, that there are many points of view on every subject. Demonstrate your personal integrity by showing your audience that you have taken the time to try and understand those points of view, even if you do not agree with them. People who are so enthusiastically headstrong about their own perspective that they don't acknowledge and respect a variety of viewpoints in every audience are usually called fanatics. Don't be a fanatic! Remember what the first century orator and philosopher, Seneca, once said, "He who comes to a conclusion when the other side is unheard, may have been just in his conclusion, but yet has not been just in his conduct"

Practice What You Preach: Speakers worth their weight in metaphors must be able to show their audience that they are willing to follow their own advice. For example, if you are talking on the subject of good dietary practices, you will need to tell your audience how you changed some of your eating habits (humility) and how those changes have affected you.

Share Your Own Experience: Speakers who want to gain an audience's trust, will need to put themselves in the picture. Share a personal story but don't make yourself the hero. Show them that you have been there, too. For example, you may give your audience 101 good reasons why smoking cigarettes is not good for your health, but the magic moment of trust and respect really happens when you share with the audience about your own struggles with tobacco or when you grant them access to your personal tragedy of a loved one who died due to lung cancer. It is then, and often only then, that the people in the audience feel they can trust you enough to listen to you at a level of any consequence.

2. Friendliness

If we want an audience to be friendly toward us or toward our ideas, then we ought to be friendly toward the audience. If we want an audience to like us, we will need to show the people in the audience that we like them. We can enhance our own spirit of benevolence toward an audience in a variety of important ways.

Smile: An extremely bright teenager once said to me, "Dr. Mark, if your heart feels like smiling, why not inform your face?" If we want the audience to know that we are glad for the opportunity to be with them on a particular occasion, one of the ways we can communicate that feeling, apart from our words, is with a smile. When speakers don't smile, it sends out negative messages to their audiences. But when they smile, it is one of the clearest ways of saying, "Thanks for having me. I'm glad to be here with you." As the old saying goes, "Smile and the whole world smiles with you." When you smile, you can make an audience feel great. And who doesn't like feeling great. Think of an audience like a mirror. When you face them with a smile, they smile right back! And next time they do, don't get too smug, just smile and say to your self, "Hey, I did that."

Make Eye Contact: By making eye contact and lots of it, you tell your audience that you respect them enough to look them in the eyes and you tell them that you respect them enough not to hide behind your notes. The eyes, it has been said, are the window to the soul. Why not open up the window and share a bit of yourself with the audience?

Share Your Feelings As Well As Your Ideas: Quite often people, particularly younger people, care less about what you know and more about how you feel. Information is important. Even necessary. However, people can read books and get information. In a

A word to the wise: If you can avoid it, never start a speech with an apology. An apology, whether for having a sore throat, being nervous, or anything else, focuses the audience's attention on the negative rather than the positive.

speech, you have an opportunity to bring in more feeling with your information. People tend to make a stronger connection when someone shares their feelings about a particular subject.

Enjoy Some Appropriate Laughter: Humor is an effective way to get an audience to warm up to you and your ideas. Almost everybody likes to laugh. And we tend to like spending time with those people who can make us laugh. Just make sure it is not humor at their expense. Nobody likes a speaker who puts down an audience. Instead, without being uncomfortably self-deprecating, show the audience that you are not above laughing at yourself. Use humor to lighten the mood or relax your audience. But remember, if you just aren't funny, don't try to be.

Be Human, Be Humble and Be Real! The more we live in an automated and technical world, the more we look for genuinely human encounters. One of the best ways of building ethos with an audience is by being authentic. Take some risks. Share some of your own failings or shortcomings. Your audience knows that you are not perfect. They just want to know that you know it too! Too much bravado or cockiness can turn-off an audience. Just relax. You have nothing to prove except your respect for your audience.

3. Competence

While your audience will be reluctant to listen to someone who is oozing arrogance, it will also be cautious about tuning in to someone who appears incompetent. People are busy. People are impatient and sometimes even angered by speakers who waste their time. A lack of preparation and/or practice can turn an audience cold and, not to mention, make us look like bumbling idiots! The three Ps of competency are: Preparation, Practice and Personal Appearance.

Preparation. The most competent speakers know enough about speaking to be prepared. There are two important elements of preparation:

First, being prepared means doing your homework. Know the issues at hand. Understand the latest developments in the study of your subject. No matter how much you think you already know about a particular subject, research is absolutely necessary. The more you have researched and the better you understand your research, the more comfortable you will be and the more competent you will sound to your audience.

Show your audience how competent you are by documenting your research. You don't have to read them a bibliography, but a simple citation telling your audience where your quote or statistic came from will make you appear accountable, trustworthy and professional.

Secondly, being prepared means having a well thought out plan of attack—a design or structure for your speech. Speakers who wander aimlessly without focus can quickly frustrate an audience. We have all experienced far too many speeches where the speaker thought he or she could just "wing it" but in the end made a mess out of things.

Imagine a film maker who just starts shooting the camera, collects all sorts of images, ideas, even scenes but has no idea where the film is headed, avoids editing all together and just starts playing back the film for the audience. Now that's a disaster film! Without story boards and plot, or design and editing, the film would likely do little more than just anger or frustrate the audience. The effect is generally the same for those speeches that just take off without a direction. Instead of insulting your audience with a lack of direction, build ethos with a clear plan of attack!

Practice. I can hardly stress enough the importance of practicing your speech. The more comfortable you are with its content and design, the more competent you will appear before your audience. The more you know where it is going, the less dependent you will be on your notes. The less dependent you are on your notes, the more eye contact you can make. The more eye contact you make, the more competent you will appear. This is one of the most overlooked elements of speech writing—learning the speech. A well-rehearsed speech can make the difference between a bad speech and a great one! Practice it by yourself many times. Then practice your speech in front of some friends or your family. Don't worry that they might laugh. They are probably nervous, too!

Personal Appearance. One of the most overlooked aspects of student speeches is our personal appearance. Speakers who dress respectfully, generally receive respect—even before they start speaking!

I once had a student who forgot it was speech day and had to deliver his speech in his cut-offs and a sleeveless basketball shirt. Even though he had apologized about his attire, his peers did not respond to his speech in the way they should have. His casual wear sent out a negative message: "I really don't care enough about you [the audience] to have taken the time to dress for the occasion." The apology sent out the same kind of message: "I didn't care enough about you, the audience, or this assignment to remember that it was due today." Other students had prepared, practiced and paid close attention to their personal appearance. His disregard for his own personal presentation turned his speech into a bit of a flop. The general rule here is let the attire match the formality of the occasion and always dress just a little better than your audience.

> In a nutshell, those speakers who seem most competent are th ose who are prepared, practiced, and dressed respectfully for the occasion.

4. Dynamic Presence

We will talk specifically about vocal production later, but for now let's just say that a great delivery can greatly enhance your credibility with an audience. The word dynamic comes from the Greek word *dunamis* which, literally translated, means power. Dunamis is also the word from which we get the modern English term, dynamite. To have a dynamic presence as a public speaker, we not only need to know what we are talking about, we need to sound like it too!

Be Enthusiastic. The kind of energy you bring to your speech will greatly enhance your believability as a speaker. If you're not excited your speech, most definitely your audience won't be either. Your enthusiasm endorses your message.

Be Clear. Audiences appreciate speakers who can be heard and speakers who can be understood. There is an old saying, "If a bugle gives an indistinct sound, who will get ready for battle?" (1 Corinthians 14:8, Holy Bible). As a speaker, you cannot afford to give an indistinct sound. You need to say it loud and say it proud.

Be Confident Not Arrogant. No one in your audience knows exactly how you are feeling. Only you. No one can see how fast your heart is beating. No one can feel how clammy your hands might be. Even blushing cheeks never appear as rosy-red to the audience as they feel to you. You don't need to show your audience that you are nervous. As we learned in the last chapter, even if we have an ugly dog, we can still walk it proudly!

The more self-assured you appear, the more relaxed the audience will be. And not only will acting confident relax your audience, but when you see the audience relax, in turn, you will become more at ease. Don't be a phony, but why show the audience all your cards.

Fake It 'til You Make It . If you can fake it long enough, in time you will find yourself building self-confidence and becoming more relaxed as a speaker. Faking it in the beginning allows you the opportunity to get in some well-needed practice as a speaker. In her article entitled Speak Up About Speech Anxiety (*The Campus Chronicle,* 09/26/03), Sophie Viola, a counselor for the Savannah College of Art and Design, reminded her readers that "speech anxiety causes people to avoid the one thing that can help them the most: experience." By faking at first, not only will you build ethos with your audience, you will have given yourself an opportunity to bank some of that all important experience.

> Ethos is the personal credibility or personal character of the speaker. Without it, we might as well gather up our numbered note cards and go home!

Upon Reflection

1. Smile. Even if nothing is particularly amusing. Just smile. How do the muscles in your face feel when you smile? How does your heart feel when you smile?
2. Name one thing that makes you smile. Why?
3. Visit http://terrabytes.virtualave.net/SmileActivities.html.
4. Visit: http://historychannel.com; click on "Audio/Video" and browse through some famous speeches. Are the speak-

ers able to establish ethos with their audiences? Listen to former New York Governor, Mario Cuomo, address the 1984 Democratic National Convention. Does he sound enthusiastic? Why or Why Not?

*Aristotle (384-322bc). Aristotle was a Greek philosopher and scientist. Aristotle was one of the most influential thinkers of the western world. He was a student of Plato and a teacher of Alexander the Great. His life's work was a rethinking and systematizing of virtually every known realm of science - from logic to ethics, from biology and physics to psychology to metaphysics. Aristotle identified three effective tools for orators: ethos (personal character of the speaker), logos (logic, reason, knowledge) and pathos (appeals to feelings). Each can be is useful, but the most powerfully persuasive speakers employ all three!

— 5 —

Introducing Yourself

You would have thought I was in confession.
I totally spilled my guts, rambling on
about this, that and the other thing.

THE YEAR WAS NINETEEN seventy-eight. I was sixteen years old and desperate for a job. I needed money for the usual sort of stuff: records, drums sticks and concert tickets. My favorite band, Queen, was coming to town and I wanted to go. So I hit the bricks and started filling out applications in local stores and restaurants. You can imagine how excited I was when one restaurant called to invite me for an interview.

I cleaned-up as well as I could. I put on a clean pair of pants and a dress shirt. Washed my face, brushed my teeth and even combed my very long and curly hair. I had all my bases covered. I was ready.

A 'By the Book' Greeting

Things seemed to be going well, at first. A kind waitress escorted me to a quiet table near the back of the restaurant and told me that the manager would be with me momentarily. When Mr. Manager arrived, I stood up, made eye contact, and then offered a cordial and confident smile as I extended my hand to offer a firm, but not too hard, handshake. Strictly by the book, here!

But then it happened. Before we had really even got started, the interview went from sweet to sour.

I was thrown off when Mr. Manager served up his opening question. It was distastefully bland. Nothing to chew on, really.

"Nice to meet you, Mark. Tell me a little bit about yourself."

I didn't know what to say about myself. I hadn't thought about how I would answer a general question like that. Oh, if he had asked me about previous work history, interest in the job, or even why I was applying to his greasy little restaurant—more specific questions—I could have easily answered. But 'Tell me about yourself?' This was far too vague.

Check Please!

You would have thought I was in confession. I totally spilled my guts rambling-on about this, that and the other thing. I mumbled pathetically about where I was born and why my parents had moved to Canada when I was three. I bumbled about my two brothers, their work history, my work history, my school, my friends and about a hundred other things which kept this potential employer wishing he had never asked the question. I had just blown the 'ice-breaker' question. "Check, please!"

A Character Only a Mother Could Love.

So sue me, I was nervous! And what I had to say, albeit a bit too much, had to be at least somewhat interesting. And sure, my voice was quiet, but some thoughtful employer might interpret this as a sign of a kind and gentle spirit, the way my mother did. But none of it mattered. In the end, I didn't get the job.

Weeks after, while reflecting on why I hadn't heard back from the manager, it dawned on me that I had not come to the interview fully prepared. True, I was wearing the right attire. And equally, true, I had come prepared to answer questions like why I wanted the job or about my limited work history—if we had ever made it that far in the interview!

But I had never been asked to introduce myself before. At least not without some sort of specific answer in mind like, "where are you from?" or "how did you hear about the job?" No, I was asked a question for which I was not prepared, and therefore, unable, to answer.

Help! What do I do?

What do we do in these sorts of situations? A job interview? A school application meeting? A first date? Or the first day of college and yet another professor asks us to stand up in front of the class and introduce ourselves? If you want to be ready, or in the very least, you don't want to sound like a mumbling, bumbling idiot who rambles into a downward verbal spiral, there are a number of things you will want to bear in mind.

Nine Important Tools for Self Introductions

1. *Plan Ahead.* Ask yourself why you will be having this particular conversation? What is pertinent information and what is not? Maybe how many fillings you have or what your favorite color is are not relevant to the goal at hand. I have listed a couple of websites at the end of this chapter that should help you with specific questions for which you might be prepared.

2. *Stay Focused.* Have an idea of what it is you really would like to say about yourself. Stick to one or two things only. Sure, you have had lots of exciting experiences and visited all sorts of cool places, but when you give people too much information about yourself, you run the risk of overwhelming or confusing your audience, or worse, you end up sounding like an ad in the personal columns: "I like moonlit walks on the beach, jazz music, candlelight dinners, snuggling under a warm blanket with my special someone . . ." The goal here is to stay on track. Don't wander.

3. *Make Connections.* Whatever you say about yourself, make sure you tell your audience why it is important to you or how it connects to the goal at hand or how it has had an effect on your life. I once had a student who introduced herself by talking about one of her favorite rock groups, The Cure. But she didn't just blather on in dreamy schoolgirl jargon about 'how cool the band is' or about their 'awesome concerts.' Instead, my student told us about her sister's interest in the band and how The Cure had given her sister some well-needed focus to deal with a clinical emotional disorder. Her speech ended creatively by saying, "In a way, the cure for my sister's disability was The Cure."

4. Practice. Once you have an idea of what it is you want to say about yourself, practice it a few times. Get comfortable with your message. You will have enough to be nervous about when the time for your self-introduction speech or interview arrives. Knowing what you want to say ahead of time will help you sound more decisive in the actual moment.

5. Be Certain. If you know what you want to say, and you have taken a little bit of time to practice saying it, you will decrease the number of times you use "uhm" or "uh" in you message. The "uhms" and "uhs" make you sound unfocused or unclear. They can produce confusion in your audience. Know what you want to say. Practice saying it. Get comfortable with silent pauses. Unless you are Billy Bob Thornton in *Swing Blade,* you don't need to fill up every break in a sentence with a grunt or an "uhm."

> As speakers, we need to connect the head and the heart.

6. Be Enthusiastic. In the last chapter we talked about how important your enthusiasm is for developing personal credibility. Don't forget, your enthusiasm endorses your message. And in the case of a self-introduction speech or an interview, you and/or your qualifications are the message. You will also want to sound enthusiastic about the context whether it is a new class you are taking, a first date or a job or college interview. Your audience will want to see that you are motivated. First impressions are critical!

7. Listen Carefully. Good communication is as much about listening as it is about speaking. Being attentive to the ideas, information and opinions of others is a sign of personal maturity, as well as a sign of respect for the people with whom you are in conversation. Be interesting and interested. Besides, talking without listening is a sure fire way of sticking your foot in your mouth.

8. Be Brief! For too many of us, our favorite subject is ourselves. When introducing yourself, take your time, but don't take too much time.

9. Visualize a Positive Outcome. Once you've put all your ducks in a row through preparation and practice, picture the interview or speech going well. Your mental preparation is important, too.

Trying to develop a singular focus for a Self-Introduction speech? Osborn and Osborn suggest choosing one category from the Self Awareness Inventory.

1. Is your cultural background the most important thing about you?
2. Is the most important thing about you the environment in which you grew up?
3. Was there some particular person – a friend, relative, or childhood hero- who had a major impact on your life?
4. Have you been shaped by some unusual experience?
5. Are you best characterized by an activity that brings meaning to your life?
6. Is the work you do a major factor in making you who you are?
7. Are you best characterized by your goals or purpose in life?
8. Are you best described by someone that you hold dear?
—Osborn and Osborn, *Public Speaking*, 5th Edition

Upon Reflection

1. Find a friend. Interview one another for your dream job. Now interview each other for your nightmare job.

2. With some friends or student peers, role-play a television or radio talk show. Develop a list of questions to ask your "guests" and have them respond.

3. Choose a category from Osborn and Osborn's, Self Awareness Inventory (above), and develop a two-minute speech that stays on track.

4. Research websites that offer tips for preparing for a job interview, including Resumagic and Hobson's College View listed below.

More Tips for Interview Preparation
Resumagic.com or other sites to help you prepare
http://www.resumagic.com/interviews_preparation.html
http://www.collegeview.com/career/interviewing/
preparation/getready.html

— 6 —

Vocal Production

Words mean more than what is set down on paper.
It takes the human voice to infuse them
with shades of deeper meaning.
—Maya Angelou

By slowing your speech down, not only do you let yourself be heard, you give the audience an opportunity to absorb and process what you are saying.

WHAT MAKES THE DIFFERENCE between a good speech and a great speech? Simply put: the voice. Our voices are the most underused tools in our speaker's toolbox. We may have written an excellent speech, filled with brilliant metaphors, poignant allegories and subtle euphemisms. Our speech design may be constructed in a simple and easy to follow manner. We may even have an introduction that will capture audience attention and a conclusion that ties the speech together neatly. But if we are unable to use our voice effectively, our good speech runs the risk of being inefficacious.

Previously, I told you about a bright teenager who once said to me, "Mark, if your heart feels like smiling, why not inform you face." A great thought, indeed. But the very same thing can be said about the voice: *If your heart feels like smiling, why not inform your voice!* As speakers, we need to connect the heart and the head. Everything we say has a value attached to it, positive or negative. That value ought to be reflected, to one degree or another, through our voices. It is true that words themselves carry meaning, but as Maya Angelou so aptly stated, it is our human voice that brings shades of deeper meaning to the words we have set down on paper. If our ultimate goal is to inspire within our audience, understanding and, possibly, agreement and action, in the case of persuasive speaking, then making the best possible use of our voices is mandatory. It is, in fact, one of the most critical components to a great speech!

Ten Tips for Great Vocal Production

1. Volume. Clearly one of the greatest difficulties for many novice speakers is being heard. Sadly, I have heard, or rather, I have barely heard, many speeches that were written well but which fell on deaf ears because no one could hear what was being said. Often we are shy about our own thoughts. We are afraid of making a fool of ourselves or saying the wrong thing so we hold back. You may want to revisit Chapter Three for tips on dealing with your communication apprehension.

Say it loud and say it proud! What you have to say is worth hearing!

If you have done that, then try taking some slow, deep breaths —in through the nose and slowly out from the mouth—before you start speaking. Relaxing yourself is very important.

When you are ready to speak, fill your lungs with air, tighten the belly slightly so that it can help you push air up from the diaphragm. Create a slight resistance in the voice so you don't let all that air escape at once otherwise, you'll have nothing left for your next sentence. Besides, it's the slight resistance that allows you to create some volume. Be careful, however, not to create so much resistance that you sound like you are in pain! Have you ever filled a balloon with air and then tightened the neck to create a shrill squeaking sound to annoy your friends and family? You don't want to do that with you voice!

2. Tempo. The second most common problem for speakers is the speed at which people deliver their speech. Most often, if tempo is the issue, the speech is too fast. Some speakers will stand in front of their audience and race through their notes like an auctioneer taking bids on market day! Sometimes they are eager to get it over with, other times they are just plain nervous that what they have said may not please the audience so they rush to get on to their next point.

Here are two things that might help you if you are having trouble putting on the brakes: *Relax, and don't read your speech.* Again, relaxation affects so many elements concerning vocal production. If you are still having trouble relaxing, go back to Chapter Three and see if you missed something.

We read so much more quickly than we speak. Practice your speech ahead of time enough to be comfortable with where you want to go and what you want to say without memorizing it (memorizing your speech verbatim is a recipe for stress—besides, you end up reading it to us off the pages in your mind's eye anyway). Get your nose out of your notes and start talking to your audience and not at them. By talking to your audience, instead of reading your speech, you will slow things down greatly.

> "Just as you would never turn in an essay you knew was filled with errors, never deliver a speech filled with pronunciation errors."
> —Cindy Griffith
> Invitation to Public Speaking.

3. *Pauses.* Related to tempo, are pauses. All speakers need to pause periodically for effect to allow the audience to absorb and process what has just been said and themselves to take a breath and think about where they are going next. When I first started speaking, I used to write "PAUSE!" in bold letters throughout my speech. Over time, pausing has become a natural part of the rhythm of my speech. Get comfortable with the silence. Silence is good!

4. *Pitch and Inflection.* Pitch is a musical term that refers to the rise and fall of a musical tone. When we speak, our voice is our instrument. There ought to be a musicality to our speaking as our voice rises and falls reflecting the mood of our speech.

Inflection is the adjustment we make to pitch. Inflection moves the pitch up or down.

Without pitch and inflection our voices are as dry as whole-wheat toast! Through pitch and inflection we reduce the chance that our audience will slip into that semi-comatose world of daydreams and menu planning.

5. *Cadence.* Cadence refers specifically to the fall of a sentence or a phrase. Too often speakers allow their voice to drop off at the ends of their sentences leaving the audience straining forward to hear what was said. Can you imagine watching a film and at the end of every scene the camera fades out just seconds before the scene is fully completed. It would both frustrate and confuse us. Don't let your sentences fade out before they are finished.

6. *Pronunciation.* Practice pronouncing your words, especially if they are tricky words or come in a run of scientific jargon, or in a quote such as, "the leading recombinant bovine growth hormone (rBGH)," from David Batstone's article, "Got Milk, Just Don't Ask Where it Came From" (SojoMail, 10 29 03).

Sometimes it's the simple words that we rush through so quickly we mispronounce them. Often times, "ask" gets pronounced, "aks" and "teeth" comes out sounding like "teef." One word that I used to have trouble with was "open." When I was rushing things, I sometimes pronounced open with a slight nasal sound because I wasn't shaping the sound of the "O" with my mouth. It sounded more like "ompen." Someone pointed out my mispronunciation, and I refused to believe her. Then I heard myself on tape, and sure enough, I was mispronouncing one of the simplest words in the English language! Slow down and make sure you are pronouncing your words properly. Your credibility and your audience's understanding are both at stake.

7. *Articulation.* Articulation is similar to pronunciation, but while pronunciation is concerned with enunciating individual words, articulation has its focus on how we pronounce words within phrases and sentences. Sometimes we tend to slur words together and create confusion in our audiences. Make sure you clearly articulate each word within your phrases.

When I was a kid, my grandfather taught me the following song that if you sang it too quickly you would likely slur your words together and mispronounce a particular one which made you sound like you were swearing:

Sarah, Sarah, sitting in the shoeshine shop. She sits all day while she shines all day, She shines all day while she sits all day. Sarah, Sarah, sitting in the shoeshine shop.

Without sounding robotic, slow down and try articulating your words so that they don't bleed into one confusing sound.

8. *Passion.* Some of our most passionate words fall flat as a pancake because the voice is not reflecting the sentiment of our

Neil Young once sang, "Its better to burn out than it is to fade away!" (Hey, Hey, My, My) The same holds true when it comes to your voice: don't let your sentences fade out before they are finished.

words. Remember, it takes our human voice to bring shades of deeper meaning to our words. Passionate speakers have learned to connect the heart with the mouth. Part of the Enlightenment's downfall was that it taught us to view emotions as weaknesses, and expressions of our passion to be uncomely or embarrassing. But it is just not true. In speaking, people are moved by the passion of the speaker.

9. Conviction. Whether it is an informative speech or a persuasive one, audiences need to know that you believe what you are saying. If you sound like you believe what you are saying, chances are your audience will believe it too. I remember inviting a guest speaker from Zaire. He spoke numerous languages. English was his weakest. Although, in one-on-one conversation, he was not too difficult to follow, when he stood in front of the group of seventy or so, we could barely understand a word he said. The whole time he was speaking, I was fretting about having invited this man to speak and wondering how the audience would receive him.

After the event was over, people approached me to tell me what a great speaker he was. I couldn't believe their response. I asked a handful of people to tell me why they thought he was such a good speaker. Their reply taught me something very important about conviction: "Oh, we didn't understand a word he spoke," they confessed, "but he said it with such conviction, we knew he exactly what he meant!"

10. Enthusiasm. As we learned previously, your enthusiasm is an important tool for establishing your personal credibility—your ethos. Expressing energy and excitement with your voice will also help maintain audience attention. If you don't sound excited about your subject, why would your audience even be interested in what you have to say? But if your voice expresses enthusiasm about having the opportunity to speak and enthusiasm for your subject, chances are your audience will be, in the very least, attentive and interested.

Upon Reflection

1. Choose a children's story and read it as if you are trying maintain the attention of an unruly class of first graders.

2. Better yet, find an unruly group of children and read them your children's story!

3. Connect to www.historychannel.com. Click on video/audio. Sample some speeches and compare how a variety of speakers are using the voice.

4. Try out a few tongue twisters on the following Tongue Twister Fun page or visit the suggested sites.

Tongue Twisters!

Tongue twisters are a great way of loosening up the voice before a speech. Practice a few of these tongue twisters, applying the elements of great vocal production, and see if they help develop your speaking voice! Start slowly, and then increase your speed. Notice that in some cases, applying a rhythm helps keep the flow moving.

For more tongue twister fun, visit

The Tongue Twister Data Base at: http://www.geocities.com/Athens/8136/tonguetwisters.html

The First International Collection of Tongue Twisters at: http://www.uebersetzung.at/twister/

Try These!

Rubber baby buggy bumpers

Red leather yellow leather

How much wood, would a woodchuck chuck, if a woodchuck could chuck wood? A woodchuck, would chuck, all the wood he could chuck, if a woodchuck could chuck wood.

A skunk sat on a stump and thunk the stump stunk, but the stump thunk the skunk stunk.

Unique New York.

Betty Botter had some butter, "But," she said, "this butter's bitter. If I bake this bitter butter, it would make my batter bitter. But a bit of better butter-- that would make my batter better."

So she bought a bit of butter, better than her bitter butter, and she baked it

— 7 —

The Power of Listening

If speaking is silver, then listening is gold.
—Turkish Proverb

IF YOU WANT TO BE a great speaker, then become a great listener. At the root of good communication skills are good listening skills. The famous American psychologist, Carl Rogers, put it this way: "Man's inability to communicate is a result of his failure to listen effectively." The skills we need in order to communicate effectively as public speakers, in many ways, depend largely on the skills we develop as listeners.

Listening not only benefits the audience; it benefits the speaker too. When we listen attentively as others speak, we are affirming their value as human beings. We send out the message that what they have to say is worth listening to. M. Scott Peck*, speaking at a conference in Detroit in the early nineteen nineties, went so far as to call listening "an act of love." Like any act of love, listening has to be intentional and it takes some effort. But when we listen with visible interest, we get more out of it and it can even help the person talking become a better speaker.

Doing the work of listening, even to bad speakers or ones that are difficult to understand, will yield amazing results both for the audience and the speaker.

Red Flags for Listeners
Sometimes its not an ear plug that is blocking our hearing, but some other issue. Here are a few common things that all of us need to watch for if we are going to listen more effectively.

Don't Judge. Sometimes we evaluate speakers before they have even said a word. We tend to evaluate the clothes they are wearing, the way their hair is combed or even the way they walk or move to the podium. Observations are fine, but if we pass judgment because of our subjective observations, we may end up blocking the speech before it starts.

Don't Stereotype. Stereotyping is a kind of judging. But it is the kind of judging we do because of a certain group to which the speaker belongs. Sometimes we will assess a speaker before he or she opens his or her mouth simply because they are a certain age or gender. I often get stereotyped because I am a minister. My students are often stereotyped as "purple-haired freaks" simply because they are art students. Other times they get stereotyped as "being spoiled, rich kids" because they go to a private school. Some of my students have even missed out on part-time job opportunities because a potential employer stereotyped them as being unreliable. Stereotyping is unfair and it hurts. Don't let your preconceived notions about someone impair your hearing.

> "Courage is what it takes to stand up and speak; courage is also what it takes to sit down and listen."
> —Winston Churchill

Don't Assume You Know What the Speaker is Going to Say. One of the biggest road blocks to our hearing a speaker, whether in conversation or in a speaking event, is the attitude that we've heard it all before and therefore, don't need to listen to what this particular speaker is going to say. Keep your ears and your mind open and you just might be surprised at what you hear!

Don't Assume You Have Heard What Has Been Said. Unless we think about what has been said or ask good questions to understand what has been said, we sometimes miss what the speaker is really trying to say. For example, when people ask me for my name, I usually spell it first: G-i-u-l-i-a-n-o. Then I pronounce it: juleeano. If I say my name first and then spell it, people generally spell it just as they have heard it. Even when I say "'G', as in George," they will write down "J." You can imagine how frustrating it is when I am dealing with the gas or phone company or the doctor's office and am continually told they don't have me on file because they keep looking under the 'js' or because when I first registered someone refused to listen to me spell my name.

They just went ahead and spelled it the way they wanted to spell it! Sometimes we may be listening, but, in fact, we are not listening carefully.

Don't Plan What You Are Going to Say While the Speaker is Still Talking. Whether it is during a speech or in a conversation, one of the greatest blocks to our hearing happens when our focus is on our response plan rather than on what the speaker is trying to say. Too often, while the person speaking is still talking, we are busily thinking about what we are going to say next or how we will refute his or her argument. If you are afraid you are going to forget your point or if there is something specific to which you want to respond, jot it down and let your notes be your memory so you can focus on what the speaker is saying.

Developing Effective Listening Skills: Before the Speech

Be Rested. If you want to hear what is being said, then you will need to have enough energy to do so. An enthusiastic audience is as important as an enthusiastic speaker!

Be Sufficiently Comfortable. Make sure you don't need to fuss and fidget your way through a speech. It's distracting to the speaker and to the people around you.

Be Clear of Distractions. Practice the courtesy of turning off your cell phone or completely clearing your space of other things that may distract others in the audience or the speaker.

Honor the Time. Make sure you don't have to sneak-in or out during someone's speech. You are never as inconspicuous as you think!

Be Comfortable with the Time. Remind yourself that you have time to listen. It is hard to hear anybody if you feel like you are in a rush. Constantly checking your watch or looking up at a clock will frustrate you and stress out the speaker. Be patient.

Be Curious. As you are getting ready to hear the speech remind yourself that you are a lifelong learner and that every human being has something of value to say. You will get something from what is being said, if you are willing to listen.

Be Ready to Take Notes If Necessary. You may be receiving

a lot of information. Notes will help you record ideas so that you can reflect on them later. Be ready before the speech so that you don't have to go digging through a packsack or whispering to someone next to you in search of a pen.

During the Speech

Focus Attention on the Speaker. In this era of multitasking, you may feel like you can do some text messaging and listen to what is being said, but you can't listen as well. M. Scott Peck has said that "You cannot truly listen to anyone and do anything else at the same time." To listen involves our whole being and, therefore, our undivided attention.

Be Fully Present. Sometimes we can be absent even though we are present. That is to say, our bodies may be in a close proximity to the speaker, but our minds have drifted off into La La Land! Daydreaming is an easy escape, but not a good tool for listening effectively.

Remain Curious and Show Your Interest. If your heart feels like smiling, why not inform your face! You can encourage a speaker simply by offering a smile, a nod of agreement or other subtle signs affirmation. As a speaker, early on in the speech, I will eye over the crowd to see who is nodding or smiling or responding to my humor or stories. These are the people who energize me with feedback and affirmation. You have an amazing power to pick up the speech simply by the way you chose to respond to the speaker.

Reflect the Speaker's Energy. A speaker's enthusiasm will increase if he or she senses that the audience is energetic and responsive. Try to reflect back to the speaker the kind of energy he or she is putting out. Sit upright and be attentive.

Make Eye Contact with the Speaker. One of the greatest ways you can show interest and offer encouragement to a speaker is by looking the speaker in the eyes. Your eyes are the window to the soul. When you make eye contact with the speaker you are increasing the level of trust and, therefore, the speaker's willingness to take more meaningful and helpful risks with his or her speech.

Don't React, Do Respond. Keep an open mind to what is being said even if you don't agree with it. By filing away your concern in a mental note or jotting it down on a piece of paper, you free up your mind to hear the rest of what was being said. When you sit and stew you miss the rest of the speech. I once had a couple angrily march out in the middle of one of my sermons. They created such a ruckus, which was probably their intention, that they threw me off balance and totally distracted the audience by interrupting the flow of the speaking moment. Had they stuck around, they would have quickly learned I was just playing the devil's advocate. Don't get bogged down in the minutia. Instead, listen to the whole message before evaluating what has been said.

Listen Even If You Don't Agree. Congresswoman Eleanor Holmes Norton (D-DC), has stated that, "the only way to make sure people you agree with can speak is to support the rights of people you don't agree with." The right to free speech is our First Amendment right. If you disagree, you will get a chance to refute after the speech is finished. Who knows, you might even develop a speech to take up the counter point!

After the Speech

Thank the Speaker and Express Your Interest. If you would like the speaker to respond favorably to your question(s) then make sure to offer up some thanks for what you received from their speech. Be specific.

Echo What Has Been Said and Ask Questions for Clarity. Before launching into a counter argument, make sure you have fully understood the speaker's position. You may be closer to agreement than you think.

Upon Reflection

1. Find a friend or classmate and try the listening challenge, *Do You Hear What I Hear?* from the page 67.

2. Next time you are at a party or public gathering, close your eyes and listen to the conversations around you. Who are the talkers and who are the listeners? Are the listeners really listening?

3. Would you say you are a better talker or a better listener?

4. Visit www.history.com and practice your listening skills while listening to some great speeches.

* M. Scott Peck, MD (b.1936) was born in New York City. A graduate of Harvard and Case Western, Peck has written numerous books in the fields of psychology, psychiatry and religion. His works include People of the Lie: The Hope For Healing Human Evil, The Different Drum: Community Making and Peace and The Road Less Traveled, which has sold over sicx million copies in North America and been translated into over twenty different languages. Dr. Peck founded the Foundation for Community Encouragement, a non-profit organization that teaches the principles of healthy community.

Do You Hear What I Hear?

To demonstrate how we have a tendency to hear what we want to hear, my colleague, Carolyn Babcock, PhD, uses the following factual listening exercise, from Interplay*, with her students.

Directions: Find a friend and ask them to write down their response to the following questions. Allow your friend enough time to answer each question but not enough time to analyze or evaluate each question. Ask each question only once.

1. How many members of each species did Moses take aboard the ark?

2. Can a man in South Carolina marry his widow's sister?

3. If a farmer lost all but nine of his 17 sheep, how many would he have remaining?

4. Does England have a fourth of July?

5. How many months have 28 days?

6. How many two-cent stamps in a dozen?

7. What was our president's name in 1970?

8. You are a baby bull. You have been away from home for a long time and are in need of loving. To whom would you go, mama bull or papa bull?

9. You are the pilot of an airliner flying between New York and Chicago. The copilot is five years younger than the pilot. The copilot's spouse is three years younger than the pilot's spouse. The interior of the plane is blue, and the seats are red. How old is the pilot?

10. A plane crashes on the border between the United States and Canada. In what country do they bury the survivors?

Answers: 1. None. Moses didn't go on the ark. It was Noah. 2. No, he would be dead. 3. Nine.. 4. Yes, it just isn't a holiday. 5. All, some just have more. 6. Twelve. 7. Same as it is now.8. Papa bull – there are no mama bulls. 9. Same age as you are. Remember, "You are the pilot . . . " 10. Survivors don't get buried.

*Interplay: The Process of Interpersonal Communication, 7th Edition. Prepared by Carol Zinner-Dolphin for Harcourt Brace & Company, 1995.

Part Three

Your Message

— 8 —

The Informative Speech

Anyone who stops learning is old, whether at twenty or eighty.
Anyone who keeps learning stays young. The greatest thing in life is to
keep your mind young.
—Henry Ford.

Those who aren't busy being born are busy dying.
Bob Dylan

OKAY, LET'S GET SOMETHING straight, right off the bat: while the function of the informative speech is to inform, its purpose isn't simply to give people more information. We use informative speech to inspire understanding and empowerment within the lives of our audience. I am writing a book on speech and public speaking not simply to flood the market and overwhelm you with more information about this particular subject, I am trying to help people understand the importance of public address, why we speak and how to do it with more comfort and ease.

Thomas Fuller, the 17th century English clergyman and historian, once said, "tis not knowing much, but what is useful, that makes a man wise." The purpose of the informative speech is to help give birth to understanding among an audience. The informative speaker acts as midwife, assisting in the birth of that new understanding among the listeners.

As a speaker, you don't just tell people what they already know. You help them understand or how to use what they know. In the old movie, Wizard of Oz, Dorothy had the ruby slippers throughout the story. She knew it. Her friends knew it. Even the

Wicked Witch of the West knew the slippers had a certain power, although she wasn't quite sure how they worked. It wasn't until the end of the film that Dorothy could understand the information she had all along.

More and more in our age of information, we experience the dilemma of having a lot of information but lacking the understanding or knowledge of how to use that information.

David Weinberger, editor of the on-line webzine, *JOHO (Journal of the Hyperlinked Organization)*, says that "the real problem with the information being provided to us in our businesses is that, for all the facts and ideas, we still have no idea what we're talking about. We don't understand what's going on in our business, our market, and our world. In fact, it'd be right to say that we already know way too much. KM [knowledge management] isn't about helping us to know more. It's about helping us to understand. Knowledge without understanding is like, well, information."

Knowledge is Recyclable

One of the best things about knowledge is that it is recyclable. The knowledge or insight one person gains can be passed along to others. Knowledge comes to me on its way to you. And it comes to you on its way to someone else. For example, when I first moved to Savannah, Georgia, I was constantly asking people for directions. I kept (and still keep) a map in the glove box of my car at all times. I needed help knowing how to get places in this historic, coastal city, which often follows the confusing contours of the rivers and marshes more often than Oglethorpe's historic urban grid of city squares.

But now that I have lived here in 'the garden of good and evil' for a while, I am able to pass on my directional knowledge to others as they learn the city's layout. I am recycling the personal knowledge I have gained trying to find my way around Savannah. The English Philosopher, John Locke, once said that, "the improvement of understanding is for two ends: first, our own increase of knowledge; secondly, to enable us to deliver that knowledge to others." Knowledge is meant to be recycled.

Knowledge is Expandable

When we disseminate knowledge, often we augment understanding. When we share knowledge we are actually contributing to a very large, somewhat nebulous thing called a "body of knowledge." A body of knowledge is what we collectively know or understand about certain issues, philosophies or sciences. There is a body of knowledge pertaining to thermal dynamics and another pertaining to nuclear medicine. Other bodies of knowledge are concerned with the history of art, the evolution of human beings, the study of God, astronomy, etc. There is a body of knowledge connected to almost everything.

What I communicate through speaking or, in writing, on the subject of oral communication, is my contribution to the bigger picture. I put it out there so that others may examine it, evaluate it, and, perhaps, even use it. And, hopefully what I have to contribute will help increase or expand the body of knowledge concerning speech and public speaking.

Alternative researcher and president of the *Oxford Muse*, Dr. Theodore Zeldin, has stated that, "Knowledge Sharing is not like sharing a cake - you do not come away with half a cake each. Knowledge Sharing is synergistic. In other words - you each enter into a conversation with a whole cake and each come away with an even bigger cake!"

What you share in an informative speech, although not necessarily original in thought or scope, has the exciting potential of helping others gain a deeper understanding of what is already known about a particular subject.

Knowledge is Filtered

It is important to remember that while knowledge is recyclable, and while it may increase as it is shared, it is also filtered before it is passed on. Did you ever play the telephone game in Scouts or at a party? You whispered something in one person's ear. That person took what they thought you said and whispered it into the next person's ear. The next person passed the information on to the next person and so on until the message had been shared throughout the group. By the time it reached the last person, however, the message didn't sound anything like what it had started out to be. Somewhere along the way, the message was unintentionally or intentionally distorted. That's the filtration of information.

The filtration process works something like this: You hear or read information. You internalize and process that information based on your own personal knowledge and experience and then, in turn, pass that information along to others. But you are selective in what you hear. You are also selective in what you choose to pass on to others. In a sense, you are a filter through which knowledge is circulated. You can't help it. Everyone filters knowledge.

I first began to notice this process when, as a small child, I was looking at a painting on the wall. It dawned on me that since not every person has the same set of eyes, not everyone will see the same thing. The picture will look different to each of us. As I got older it became clearer and, sometimes, even a little bit frustrating. I am sure you have experienced the same thing. At family gatherings, my brothers and I would recount past family experiences. And even though each of us had experienced the same thing, we didn't always remember or it or retell it in the same way. Sometimes, it seemed that we remembered or recounted stories in such a way that the storyteller looked like the smart one and other brothers looked ridiculous. Such is the subjective filtration process. Ask ten people who witnessed an automobile accident to recount the details and you will likely get ten slightly different stories.

When we claim to be simply sharing objective truth or facts, we have not acknowledged the above subjective filtration process. Acknowledging the process helps us understand why we have heard certain things the way we have or why we are passing on the knowledge we are. Acknowledging the subjective filtration process helps us be more ethical and less dangerous in our speaking by being up front and clear about our personal agendas with audiences. Acknowledging this process helps us clarify for our audiences and ourselves just why it is we are sharing certain knowledge.

Knowledge is Edited

Being clear about our own subjective interpretation of knowledge will help us make the important decisions about what information to share and what information not to share. After all, we live in a day and age of information overload, an era when information is disseminated like pellets from a shotgun blast. We are inundated by telephone solicitors, Internet "spam" and pop-ups, television and radio advertisements, even information from professors and textbooks. As informative speakers, we don't want to overwhelm audiences with superfluous data.

Have you ever seen the spitter? The person who tries to say too much, too quickly and ends up spitting out his or her words—literally! We usually respond by saying something playful but to the point like, "Hey buddy, 'Say it. Don't spray it!'" The same adage could be applied to information and knowledge. We don't want to saturate our audience with more information than they can handle. We live in an age when people already have too much information. The general rule for informative speakers is "Say it, Don't spray it!"

Sometimes we have far more information than we need to share and editing is required. The best speakers, on behalf of their audiences, and in the name of clarity, know how to limit what they say. When speeches are concerned, often times, less is more!

A Story—No Bull!

There is a great old story about a country preacher who shows up to church one Sunday to discover that only one couple has come to worship—an old farmer and his wife. The preacher looks at his minute congregation and says, "Well, I have prepared an excellent sermon for you today, but since there are just two of you, I don't know whether I should preach it or not." The farmer looks up at the preacher who is looking a little lost in the pulpit and replies, "Well Reverend, if it was feeding time on my farm and only two of the cows came into the barn, I'd still give them something to eat." The preacher rubs his chin and says to himself, "Obviously, this couple has come a long way to be at church and they have come hungry for the word of God. So I better feed them well." The preacher smiles, gives a knowing nod to the farmer and his wife and preaches a full and robust sermon that lasts 30 minutes long.

After the service is over the preacher steps out of the pulpit and walks over to the couple to greet them. Feeling rather proud of his sermon he asks the farmer and his wife what they thought of the message. At which the old farmer, still a little drowsy after the long sermon replies, "It was a pretty good sermon, Reverend, but if just two of my cows came into the barn at feeding time, I sure wouldn't give them a whole herd's worth!"

One of the most important steps in informative speaking is deciding which information and how much of it should be used in a speech. You still need to do a thorough job of researching your materials. You just don't need to give all your information to your audience. As one of my professors used to say, "Do your homework; just don't show it all to your audience."

The Informative Speech

Now here is a statement that will make you wonder why you bought this book: The function of an informative speech is to inform. Sounds pretty simple, doesn't it? But I want to make it clear that the informative speech is not about persuading people to act or think in a new ways, rather its purpose is simply to introduce new ideas or understanding. Persuasive speakers advocate. Informative speakers educate.

As an informative speaker you act less like an advocate of a position and more like a teacher of a subject. You will likely use your skills as a communicator to motivate an audience to listen to your information, but you won't employ the tools of persuasion to get your audience to accept a particular idea or carry out a specific action. Keep it clear: your job as an informative speaker is simply to share information that inspires understanding and empowerment among the members of your audience.

That being said, as a byproduct of new knowledge, your audience may be inclined to think or act differently. I have had students teach classroom audiences about subjects such as vegetarianism. And even though they acted as teachers and not persuaders, some students had an increased interest in this subject and wanted to know more, perhaps even try it out for themselves. But that was only a byproduct of the information they received. The speaker did not try and persuade the audience to do anything other than listen and learn.

Three Types of Informative Speeches

Speeches that Describe. Speeches that describe are used when speakers are informing audiences about people, places, things or events. The table below shows examples such of speeches.

People	Places	Things	Events
Jimi Hendrix Arnold Schwarzenegger Stephen King Sallvador Dali Teenagers	The CN Tower (Toronto) Summer Cottage New York City The Detroit Institute of Art	VW Beetle Reebok Pump Statue of Liberty	Kyoto Accord G8 Summit Wide Spread Panic concert Giving Birth

Speeches that Demonstrate. There is an ancient Chinese proverb that states, "I hear and I forget. I see and I remember. I do and I understand." Speeches that demonstrate are the "how to" or "how it's done" speeches. These speeches demonstrate to audiences how to do something or how something works. In the table below are some examples of speeches that demonstrate.

How To	How It Works
Juggle Cook Thai Noodles Hula Hoop Flirt	The Electoral College The Television Internal Combustion Engine Comfort Food's Effects on the Brain

Speeches that Explain. Speeches that explain are used when the subject about which we are speaking is abstract. We would use a speech that explains when we are talking about theories, issues, or principles, as well. In the table below are some examples of speeches that explain.

Theories	Issues	Principles
Evolution/Creationism	Gun Violence in America	Supply and Demand
Quantum Physics	Stem Cell Research	Quakers
Adolescent Psychology	Poverty	Buddhism
Black Holes	Globalization	Dogma Films

The Medium is the Message*

It is not only what we say which carries meaning, but how we say it. The design we choose for our speeches is like the vehicle that carries the content we hope to deliver to the audience. Not only does the content inspire understanding within our audience, but also the specific design we choose to deliver knowledge.

The Canadian communication theorist, Marshall McLuhan*, helped us understand just how important the vehicle of communication is when he said "the medium is the message." He even went so far as to say that in some cases, particularly the case of electronic media, the medium is more important than the content itself.

Suffice it to say, the message is dependent on the medium; or that the content of our speech is useful only inasmuch as it is contained in the appropriate vehicle for delivery. Simply put, by choosing the right speech design, you can enhance understanding greatly.

For example, if I am going to deliver a descriptive type speech on the unfolding events which led up to the Battle of Gettysburg, it would help my content out greatly if I packaged it in a chronological design, describing how one event led to another or how two events were happening simultaneously. If I were going to use a descriptive type design to describe the actual setting of the battle of Gettysburg, I probably would steer away from chronology as my main focus and package the content of my speech in a spatial design, describing the actual space (location) of the battle. The content of our message will be strengthened by the design we choose to deliver it.

Six Designs for Informative Speeches

Spatial. The spatial design is useful when describing a space, place or sometimes, even a thing. If you were using a descriptive type speech to describe the interior the Detroit Institute of Art (DIA), you would probably use a spatial design. Remember, though, even space has a logical sequence to it. A rough draft of your speech design, minus introduction and conclusion, might look something like this:

1. Describe exterior of building.
    a. architecture of period
    b. use quote from *Architectural Digest* about DIA
    c. patina roof
2. Describe overwhelming impressions: massive entrance
    a. Use quote from Da Vinci: "All our knowledge has its origins in our perceptions."
    b. Perceptions upon entering through heavy doors, expansive and gleaming marble floors, soaring ceilings—a sense that new knowledge was beginning for you.
    c. Statistic about number of people who walk through that foyer each day or every year to experience the same thing.
3. Describe the main atrium, particularly Diego Rivera Murals
    a. Diego Rivera murals depicting the evolution of the auto industry in America
    b. Why Rivera was commissioned to paint the murals - possibly a quote from curator or Rivera himself.
    c. statistics about paintings—size, time it took to paint, cost, etc., possibly a quote from Henry Ford.

Chronological. Simply put, a chronological speech design describes events in the order in which they happen. This design is particularly useful for both descriptive and demonstrative types of informative speech. A rough chronological design for a demonstrative speech on juggling might be organized in the following way.

1. Getting comfortable tossing the first ball
   a. hand positions: tossing hand and catching hand
   b. arcing the ball in the right place
   c. allowing ball to fall into hand rather than reaching out to grab it. Important note: Practice this step until comfortable and confident!
2. Practicing with two balls
   a. when to throw the second ball
   b. arcing both balls in the right place
   c. catching
3. Introducing the third ball
   a. how to hold two balls in one hand
   b. when to throw balls
   c. taking the risk to try it!

Please note that, in a demonstrative speech there is plenty of room to spice it up with interesting facts and quotes. In the above example, while demonstrating how it is done, you might intersperse interesting facts about the history of juggling, the average time it takes a person to learn, juggling associations, etc.

Topical. Topical organization is one of the easiest designs to work with. It is simply organizing your informative speech into topics or categories. You might organize a speech on watercolor painting in the following topical way.

1. Properties
   a. workability
   b. dry time
   c. blending properties

2. Tools and Supplies needed
    a. types of brushes
    b. types of canvasses
3. Techniques
    a. standard or conventional brush techniques
    b. bleeding the canvass
    c. new or innovative approaches

Comparative. A comparative design for informative speech simply compares things. One thing to bear in mind, however, comparative design is a bit of a hybrid design in that it usually involves combining it with other designs. That makes it a little slippery to handle. Even though you may be comparing things, you will need to establish consistent categories within each topic to compare. For example, you may be comparing your three favorite, early Johnny Depp movies, but it will keep your subject clear to you and your audience if you identify three categories or elements within these films to compare such as acting, storyline and directing. See the example below. Note: this example is also chronological in its ordering.

1. What's Eating Gilbert Grape (1993)
    a. acting
    b. storyline
    c. directing
2. Ed Wood (1994)
    a. acting
    b. storyline
    c. directing
3. Fear and Loathing in Las Vegas (1998)
    a. acting
    b. storyline
    c. directing

Cause-Effect. A causational design is most helpful when your informative speech is concerned with causes and effects. It answers one of two questions: What caused it? or What will it cause? See the rough outline on the subject of air pollution and its effects on human beings below:

1. Cause One: Increased use of fossil fuels
2. Cause Two: Lax laws on toxic emissions for both private consumers and corporate industry
3. Effect: Increase in incidents of skin and lung cancers, and other respiratory diseases such as asthma.

Acronym. An acronym is a word that is formed by the initial letters in a series of other words. Each letter in the acronym can form a point in your speech as in following example from a demonstrative speech whose goal was to teach people How to Flirt:

C.R.E.S.T. (It whitens and it brightens!)
  C is for Confidence.
  R is for Relax.
  E is for Eye contact.
  S is for Smile.
  T is for Talk   .

If your acronym is not too long, it can form an imaginative and neat structure for a speech.

Upon Reflection

1. Visit and explore the Gurteen Knowledge website at: http://www.gurteen.com.
2. List three things you have learned from someone and then recycled by passing that knowledge on to another person.
3. Think of your favorite place and describe it spatially.
4. Choose a significant event and describe it chronologically.
5. Compare the town or city in which you now live to the

town or city in which you grew up. (Remember, pick categories to compare).

6. Try this experiment: Write a two-minute speech about your favorite pastime on your computer. Write the speech a second time. The second time, however, write the speech with a nice pen on a piece of vellum or in a journal. Did the medium shape the message?

*Marshall McLuhan (1911-1980). McLuhan, the Canadian communication theorist and critic of culture, left the world with such influential works as The Gutenberg Galaxy (1962), Understanding Media (1964) and The Medium is the Message (1967). His greatest achievement was to help us understand how the technology of communication, such as print and electronic media, shapes our understanding of the world. He showed how print communication, a language of the individual, shaped the enlightenment period and how, electronic media, will shape the next historical epoch by fragmenting society. For a more thorough biography, visit: http://www.kirjasto.sci.fi/mcluhan.htm.

— 9 —

Clarity and Design

There are basically two kinds of public speakers: those who can talk endlessly on any subject and those who can talk endlessly without a subject!

AUDIENCES NEED US TO be clear about what we are saying and how we are saying it. A speech is not like a book or an article where the reader can go back a paragraph or two and reread a section if she or he has missed something. The speaker is the one who will have to create clarity in the minds of the audience members.

When Clarity Counts

A few years back, there was a television commercial for a cell phone company. Maybe you remember it. The scene is a busy city street. On one side of the street, there is a suited man beside bus shelter. He is jumping up and down, waving frantically at another man standing on the opposite side of the road. That man is obviously confused by what he sees. He does not understand what the frantic man in the suit is so worked up about. He shrugs his shoulders, as if to say, "I have no idea what you are saying."

The man by the bus shelter then attempts yelling something across the bustling road, but his urgent words gets swallowed up in the cacophony of screeching cars and buses roaring down the road. The puzzled man on the opposite side of the street is still shrugging his shoulders in confusion.

Finally, the suited man by the bus shelter gets an idea. He grabs a large white sheet of paper and, with his trusty magic marker, draws a thick but simple black arrow pointing straight up. He holds up the sign for the man across the street to see. Just in the nick of time the man looks up to see a dangling piano snap free from a rope. He dashes out of harm's way as the piano crashes down in the very spot where he had just been standing.

At this point in the advertisement, three simple but powerful words scroll across the screen: *when clarity counts*.

In oral communication, particularly in public speaking, clarity always counts. And, as is in the illustration above, the way we often achieve clarity is with simple and clear lines of communication. If the members of your audience are shrugging their shoulders in confusion, as if to say, "we have no idea what you are saying," perhaps you need to ask yourself a couple of questions: "Is it clear to me what I want to say to my audience?" and "Are my thoughts organized simply enough that my audience will find my speech easy to follow?"

Probably the most common adage of public speaking is: Tell them what you're going to tell them. Tell them. And then tell them what you told them. This maxim of oration may sound overly simple but simplicity is precisely what you are aiming for when clarity counts. Some of the most complex processes and theories can be taught only when they are organized and delivered, simply and clearly.

> Sometimes a statement of purpose may be presented as a question to be answered or an itch to be scratched. Just make sure both you and your audience have a sense that you have a purposeful and intentional plan in mind.

In my experience as a speaker and as a teacher of speakers, if we are not achieving clarity in our speeches we need to take a closer look at two important issues: our statement of purpose, that is, what we really want to say and the structure or design of our speech.

Statement of Purpose

Although many of us may enjoy a meandering trip across the country with no specified destination or estimated time of arrival, when it comes to a speech, a speaker who seems to have no direction, destination or sense of time frustrates us unbearably! It has been said that, "there are basically two kinds of public speakers: those who can talk endlessly on any subject and those who can talk endlessly without a subject!" Don't be the latter. Know where you are going and know how you are going to get there. The best speakers spend a great deal of time sharpening their statement of purpose before they even begin to write their speech. Your statement of purpose is the one statement that crystallizes what it is you want to say to your audience and how you are going to tell them. Having a defined statement of purpose will keep you focused as you prepare and deliver your speech.

However, don't confuse a statement of purpose with a thesis statement as you might use in an essay. Having a clearly defined statement of purpose does not mean that you need to spill all the beans in the preview statement in your introduction (see Chapter 10). You don't need to dispel all mystery or curiosity about a subject from the get-go. Too often speeches that lay out too much in the introduction can be just plain boring. The important thing is that you know what it is you want to say and how you are going to say it.

Sometimes your statement of purpose may be revealed to your audience simply as a question that is going to be answered or something you are wrestling with. You can even begin by stating that you don't have all the answers but that you have been concerned about a particular issue. Sometimes a statement of purpose may be presented as an itch that needs to be scratched.

The important thing to remember, however, is that when it comes to a statement of purpose, both you and your audience need to know that there is some sense of intentional and purposeful direction for your speech. The first century orator and philosopher, Seneca*, once said, "If one does not know to which port one is sailing, no wind is favorable." Too many speakers set sail without really knowing where they are going.

Before you begin to write your speech, the first important question you want to ask yourself and answer easily and simply, is "Where am I going with this speech?"

Where am I going?

In other words, what, specifically, do you want to say to your audience? For example, a speech on the subject of New York City is vague. What do you want to say about New York City? Do you

*Lucius Annaeus Seneca (4BC – 65AD). Seneca the Younger, dramatis, statesman and philosopher, was born in Spain. He studied Philosophy in Rome where he became the tutor and then the advisor of Nero. He was the son of Seneca the Elder, the Roman rhetorician. Seneca the Younger had a precarious career having been almost executed by Caligula, then exiled by Claudius, and in the end, accused of attempting to murder Nero, sliced open his own veins and bled and drowned himself to death in a warm pool. For more on the biography of Seneca, visit the History Net's ancient history page at: http://ancienthistory.about.com/library/bl/bl_seneca1.htm#bio. Theatre students will be interested in learning more about Seneca the Dramatist at the Theatre Database at: http://www.theatredatabase.com/ancient/seneca_001.html

want to talk about its crime? How its people are coping in with the aftermath of September 11th, 2001? Its architecture? Its history? Maybe you want to talk about why it is a great place to live. You cannot talk about it all. You must decide before you begin to put pen to paper or keys to processor. Once you decide on your specific topic, the next important question you will need to ask is, "how am I going to get there?"

How am I going to get there?

Once you have identified your specific topic and begun the brainstorming process (see below) you will need to chose and be clear about which kind of design you will use to transport your ideas to your audience. Remember, in the last chapter we learned about six different designs for informative speaking: spatial, chronological, topical, comparative, cause-effect, or even, acronym. Which one best suits your purpose?

Design

Let's look at three important ways you can keep your speech designs simple and clear for both you and your audience.

One of the ways speakers achieve clarity in a speech is through an interesting but simple design. Some speakers like to think of the design of a speech like the frame of a house—unless it is well-planned in advance, the rest of the project will never work. It doesn't matter what you add to it later, it will always seem confusing.

Another way of understanding design, to continue the metaphor from the previous chapter, is to think of your speech design as the vehicle you use to transport your ideas to your audience. One vehicle may be better than another for your particular purpose.

Like the time my wife and I got our little Volkswagen Rabbit stuck in some sand when we went off-road touring up in Labrador, Canada. Miles from anywhere, we were stuck—going nowhere, fast. We jammed cardboard under the tires, floor mats and even branches from nearby scrub bushes trying to get some traction to get us moving again. But it didn't work. We had chosen the wrong vehicle to start with and in the end were forced to dig our way out. All the while, we were wishing we had taken our little trip in an SUV or a jeep or any other vehicle more suited for off-road driving. Through brainstorming your topic, you will be able to choose more easily which vehicle will be best suited to carry your ideas to your audience.

> A speech design is the vehicle we use to transport our ideas to our audience. Each vehicle has a specific purpose. Some vehicles are better suited than others for certain kinds of travel.

Simplify the Number of Points—Brainstorming

Limit the Number of Points. Often we feel we have many points to make. But given time constraints, unless we limit the number of points we are making, we usually end up doing two things. First, since we don't have time to fully develop our ideas, we end up with a list of underdeveloped ideas instead of a speech. Secondly, because there are too many ideas, and because they are underdeveloped, we end up overwhelming our audience with too much information. By limiting the number of points in a speech, we give ourselves time to fully develop our ideas and our audience the time to absorb and understand what we are saying.

In a simple speech, a properly developed supporting point (see "Simplify with a Clear Point Structure" later in this chapter), takes an average of at least one and a half to two minutes. If you

Why New York City Is a Great Place to Live

BRAINSTORMING	GROUP IDEAS

• Statue of Liberty
• Broadway
• Taxi Cabs
• David Letterman Show
• Central Park
• Mounted Police
• Restaurants
• New York Rangers
• New York Yankees
• Empire State Building
• The Museum of Modern Art
• The Guggenheim
• Muggings are down
• Murder Rate is down
• Artists Network
• Subway system
• Macy's Thanksgiving Day Parade
• Carnegie Hall
• Radio City Music Hall
• Times Square
• Small Independent Art Galleries
	1. Nightlife
	  • Broadway
	  • Restaurants
	  • Crime at an all time low
	
	2. Art Scene
	  • Museum of Modern Art
	  • Guggenheim
	  • Artists' Network
	  • Independent Galleries
	
	3. Sports Scene
	  • Yankees
	  • Rangers
	
	4. Tourist Attractions
	  • Statue of Liberty
	  • Empire State Building
	  • Macy's Thanksgiving Day Parade

are giving a five to seven minute speech, you should be limiting the number of your points to three. If you have five or six points to make in a five to seven minute speech, you are not fully developing your ideas.

Begin by brainstorming all the possible ideas for a particular subject. Don't worry about editing or evaluating ideas yet. Simply write all the things that come to mind down one side of a sheet of paper. Once you have made an extensive list, start paring down the list by removing those items that aren't absolutely necessary. Or simply choose three that you feel are most important. In most cases, less is more!

Group Your Points. During the brainstorming process, you will probably notice that some of the ideas that you have listed in one column on your paper have a commonality. Many skilled speakers will find those ideas that are similar and group them into one point, as in the example about New York City on the opposite page. In this example, you can see how much easier it would be for an audience to follow along if you, the speaker, grouped your list of ideas into the Four Best Things about Living in New York City: the Nightlife, the Arts Scene, the Sports Scene and all those amazing Tourist Attractions. Depending on the time allotted, you might even decide to drop one of your categories. As you will remember from our last chapter, this is called a Topical or Categorical design. Follow the same sort of brainstorming/grouping process regardless of the design you are using (Spatial, Chronological, Topical, Comparative, Causational, see Chapter 8).

Remember, too, that you will still want to develop each grouping or category into a supporting point structure with quotes, facts, statistics, etc. After all, a speech is so much more than just listing ideas!

Simplify with a clear point structure

Once you have grouped your ideas into main points, the next step will be to develop each point into simple and clear point structure. A point structure has a beginning (transitional statement), a middle (supporting information or evidence) and an end (closure). Structurally speaking, your point should look something like this:

> Point Structure
> 1. Transitional Statement
>   a. Supporting fact or quote, statistic, analogy, etc.
>   b. Example, expert testimony, illustration, etc.
>   c. Personal narrative, other example or illustration
> 2. Summary Statement

Transitional Statement

Every point must begin with some sort of transitional statement. The transitional statement is your opportunity to tell your audience the particular point you are about to make. It helps you transition from one point to the next by connecting your previous point and previewing the upcoming one. Don't launch into the substance of your point until you have creatively and effectively informed your audience about the point you are trying to make.

For example, if you are giving a speech entitled, In the Heart of the Empire: Living in New York City to a group of college students and your first supporting point is the nightlife, the transitional statement you use to begin your first point might be something like the following example:

1. First and foremost, New York City is a place for people who love the nightlife. When I was in the 10th grade, my girlfriend always had to be home by 11:00pm. When I got up the nerve to ask her mother about that rule, she told me that "young people will do things after 11:00pm that they would never consider doing before 11:00pm." Well I bet there are a lot of unhappy mothers in New York City. You see, New York is the 'city that never sleeps.' It has an unbeatable nightlife that keeps millions of citizens and tourists hopping from dance bar to comedy club, from rock concert to intimate jazz spot, every night. In New York City, it is nighttime fun—from dusk to dawn!

Remember, this example is not the introduction to the Speech, itself. We will get to Introductions and Conclusions in our next chapter. The example above simply exemplifies a good transitional statement into the first point of the speech.

Supporting Your Point

The middle of your point is the substance of your idea. It is the facts, quotes, statistics, illustrations, expert testimonies, personal narratives, analogies and examples that support your point. When you are sure your audience understands what your point is about, then you are ready to proceed to the middle section and substantiate your supposition as in the example below:

> A. *A-Z Travel Guide says that, "the cliché, 'the city that never sleeps' really rings true in New York, especially in Manhattan." The guide says that Manhattan Island "buzzes with nefarious nocturnal activity, with everything from bustling neighborhood bars and glitzy Broadway shows, right through to funky style bars and ultra hip nightclubs, where some of the worlds best DJs entertain the city's beautiful people."*
>
> B. *Listen to what the locals say, "If you can't find it here, you're just not looking." You can find it all in New York City: the usual stuff like movie theaters and coffee houses, and the not so usual like the Roxy which serves up Drag Queens and house music to an appreciative gay and lesbian crowd.*
>
> C. *On a recent trip to NYC, I was almost overwhelmed by the diversity of nightlife. In just one night, I heard the legendary New York house DJ, Roger Sanchez, at the alcohol free, Vinyl 6, then fellow New York clubbing giant, Eric Morillo at the CentroFly, and then finally rounded-off the experience soaking up jazz until dawn at 27 Standard on East 27th.*

Notice that there are three components of supporting evidence here (A, B, and C). You don't always have to have three, but you should never have more than three. This has to do with the timing of each point and the ability to maintain the audience's attention for the duration of that point. This became clear to both speaker and audience in Atlanta a few years back. A friend of mine was listening to a speaker in an African-American church. The speaker was spending too much time on a particular point when a person in the audience shouted out, "Okay, Reverend, we got it! Move on!" Three components of supporting evidence in a five to seven minute speech should be sufficient.

Summary Statement

The summary statement of each supporting point has two important tasks. First, it reminds your audience what you have just been talking about. Secondly, it provides point closure for your audience so that you can move, succinctly and clearly, on to your next point. Your summary statement in each point must tell the audience that you are now done talking about a particular point and are now getting ready to move on to the next point. If you don't compose good closure, the point you are finishing will blur together with your next point and leave those in the audience with a "deer in the head lights" look of confusion on their faces. Closing one point is critical to beginning the next. Check out the summary statement for point one in the New York speech below:

> *So, if the nightlife is the life for you, then I suggest you take an afternoon siesta, and when you're ready and rested, venture out onto the neon streets of the city that never sleeps!*

Once you have creatively closed your first point, you are ready to transition into your second point. Read all three italicized sections of the above example as a whole unit and you will get a pretty good idea of how one complete point might sound.

Making a Finer Point with Transitional Indicators

Unlike Transitional Statements which are placed at the beginning of supporting points to connect and preview the upcoming point, Transitional Indicators occur within each point. Transitional indicators help your audience stay tuned by immediately previewing

In communication, particularly in public speaking, clarity always counts.

supporting information and evidence in an interesting and imaginative way. For example, just before launching into a fact or statistic, why not tell the audience that you are about to give them a fact or statistic as in the following excellent examples? (I have put the transitional indicators in bold and italics to make them easy to spot).

> Tell them what you're going to tell them. Tell them. And then tell them what you told them.

- *Well don't just take my word for it, listen to what statistics have to say:* CBSNews.com reports that the there were almost 17,500 drunken driving deaths in 2001, up from just over16,500 in 1999.

- *Pick up the daily paper, even the headlines sound positive:* "Crime at Lowest Rate Since 1972."

- *Even the experts agree,* according to Wendy Hamilton of M.A.D.D., "The war on drunk driving is stalled."

- *Listen to what the locals say,* "If you can't find it here, you're just not looking."

Again, keeping your audience informed not only of what you are saying but how you are saying it, will help them stay connected with your speech. Transitional indicators are simple but effective ways of telling your audience what to listen for.

Sculpting Your Speech

Once you have developed all your points with solid transitional statements, support materials, internal transitional indicators and closing statements, imagine yourself as a sculptor and go back and adjust your points so they work well together, shaving off a little here or there, or adding something subtle in an early point that might be picked up or echoed later in your speech. Make sure you have created a good dynamic by varying the supporting materials in each point - some with more facts and statistics, others with illustrations and perhaps, a personal narrative. If each point follows the same pattern, for example, a quote, a fact, and an analogy, your speech will be so predictable your audience may start menu planning half way through your speech! Keep it varied.

Tie it together with a clear refrain system

One of the most effective ways of keeping an audience on track with your speech is the effective use of a refrain system. The refrain in a song is like the chorus. It's the part we sing over and over again. If we remember any of the words in a song, it is usually the chorus. A refrain in a speech works the same way. One line or phrase is used a number of times and for a number of reasons:

Staying on Track. A refrain system reminds the audience what it is you are talking about. It points them back to your main idea or statement of purpose. Remember, a speech is not like a book where an author only needs to write something once because readers have an opportunity to go back and re-read until they understand or remind themselves of the point the author is trying to make.

You might consider creating an easy to remember phrase within a point structure or one that is initiated in the introduction and then weaves its way throughout the entire speech.

In the example, Why New York City is a Great Place to Live, we used earlier in this chapter, the phrase, "the city that never sleeps," is used as an effective refrain to keep the audience focused on the first point which has to do with New York City's great night life.

Memory Retention. Sometimes refrain systems are used simply to help the audience remember an important point. There is an old adage that states, "If you want people to remember something, they need to hear it at least five times." Maybe you want an audience to remember a great quote or an important fact. If so, then consider letting that quote or fact become part of a refrain system that is used periodically throughout your speech.

For example, perhaps you are giving a speech on the subject of peer pressure and you want to encourage people to be true to themselves at an age when there are many confusing voices from peers who often give misleading counsel. You might not only start your speech with the short and familiar quote, "To thine own self be true," but you might let that quote headline each point in your speech, and then restate it in the conclusion so that by the time the speech is over, it will be firmly set in the mind of your audience:

> *So the next time you are feeling the sway of a friend or stranger who is tempting you to go to that dangerous place you know in your heart that you just don't want to go, whisper to yourself, the mantra of the self-assured: To thine own self be true!*

Heighten the Mood. Not only can a refrain system keep an audience on track and help with memory retention, but a good refrain system can help accentuate the mood of a speech. Many people have never heard Martin Luther King, Jr's famous, *I Have a Dream* speech but know of it simply because of his refrain, "I have a dream" which, although was not planned, crystallized his speech and, in many ways, the civil rights movement in the United States in the 1960s.

One cautionary note concerning refrain systems: Don't over do it. You don't want your speech to become so repetitive that it is overly predictable for your audience.

In Closing

In pubic speaking, clarity always counts. Keeping it clear for your audience begins in the brainstorming process when we limit or group our main points, then continues as we develop our points with solid transitional statements, supporting evidence, accompanying internal transitional indicators and succinct summary statements. We can even tie the whole speech together with a refrain system if it will enhance our message. Remember the old adage: Tell them what you're going to tell them. Tell them. And then tell them what you told them.

Upon Reflection

1. Brainstorm the great things about living in your hometown. Follow the process of limiting or grouping points. Choose three points and then try developing one of them into a complete supporting point.

2. Visit www.historychannel.com and listen to a segment of Martin Luther King's famous *I Have a Dream* speech. Does his improvisational refrain system serve to create focus, memory retention or heighten the emotion of the speech? Or, perhaps, all of the above?

3. Visit http://www.mecca.org/~crights/dream.html and read the complete text to MLK's *I Have a Dream* speech. Try delivering it out loud. Can you speak it aloud with a similar passion to MLK's?

---

*The Rev., Dr. Martin Luther King, Jr. (1929-1968) Martin Luther King, Jr., born at home in Atlanta, Georgia and assassinated at the Lorraine Motel in Memphis, Tennessee, was a minister, theologian and non-violent, civil rights activist. Arguably, he is the most famous speechmaker in the history of the United Sates of America. King's speeches dramatically changed the political, racial and civil landscape of America throughout the 1960s. His words and his life continue to shape perceptions in America and around the world, particularly when human rights are concerned. In the 1980s, the Irish rock group, U2, paid tribute to MLK with their song, *Pride (In the Name of Love)*: "Early morning, April 4 / Shot rings out in the Memphis sky / Free at last, they took your life / They could not take your pride."

— 10 —

Introductions and Conclusions

How many women in this audience want to stop relying on men to fix it? Or drill it? Or build it? Well listen up ladies. And you tool-challenged men, as well! I will teach you how to use a tool and how to use it properly and safely. The three most common and important tools in your toolbox are the power drill, the hammer and the screwdriver in all its various configurations. So let's get to work.
Adapted from a demonstrative speech on Tools by Beth Tiller, Savannah College of Art and Design.

ONCE YOU HAVE WRITTEN the body of your speech, whatever design you have chosen, you now have something to introduce. Your introduction and your conclusion are your opportunities to tell the audience, in imaginative and enthusiastic ways, what you are going to tell them and, once you're finished your speech, what you just told them. They are more than just mere bookends or adornments to your speech. Introductions and conclusions are powerful tools along the journey toward knowledge, understanding and, in some cases, action.

Introductions

In her book, *Invitation to Public Speaking*, Cindy Griffin says, "Introductions are like first impressions—they are important and lasting." Even the most interesting speech will fall flat on its rhetorical nose if the speaker fails to make a good first impression. If we want to make a good first impression and coax the audience to stick with us throughout the speech then three things must happen in the introduction. We need to capture the audience's attention, establish our own personal credibility as a speaker and pre-view our message. Each of these steps is critical to the speech's success. And each is equally important.

Capture Audience Attention

> What the speaker is saying: *"Good afternoon ladies and gen-tleman. Today I am going to talk to you about why New York City is a good place to live. New York City is a good place to live because . . ."*

> What the audience hears: *"Good afternoon ladies and gen-tleman. Today I am going to talk to you about why New York City is a good place to live. New York City blah, blah, blah . . ."*

If the speaker can't connect with the audience in the first sen-tence or two, people will begin to tune out very quickly. With our words and with our voices, we need to capture the audience's at-tention from the get-go. Here are nine outstanding ways you can connect with your audience and keep them from snoring through your speech!

Nine Outstanding Ways to Capture Audience Attention

1. Ask a Rhetorical Question. A rhetorical question is the kind of question that is asked more for effect than an explicit response. Asking the audience a rhetorical question is a great way to focus your audience toward your topic. Rhetorical questions demand answers, even if the answers are not spoken aloud and, therefore, demand attention from your audience. Be on your toes, though! Every now and then some people in your audience will try to an-swer your rhetorical question. If someone offers you an answer, you need to be able to handle the response. You might also ask your question and ask for a show of hands. This is a great way of involving the audience. The example at the beginning of the chap-ter started with a good rhetorical question:

*How many women in this audience want to stop relying on men
to fix it? Or drill it? Or build it? Well listen up ladies. And you
tool challenged men, as well! . . .*

2. *Thank and/or Compliment the Audience.* Pay heed to the
old adage: Flattery will get you everywhere. Don't be obvious or
sticky-sweet with Hallmark sentiment, though. People can smell
a phony a mile away. But do remember if people are going to give
you the time of day, it might go a long way with them if you offered them a little thanks for listening to you or for the opportunity to speak. You might even go so far as to pay them a compliment
on their venue or for being such an enthusiastic audience.

3. ***Talk to the Audience and not at the Audience.*** One way to
connect with your audience is to talk in the first and second person instead of the third. Don't allow yourself or the audience to be
third person, objective observers of a subject. Terms such as "I,"
"we," "you" and "us" are far more appropriate than "one," "he,"
she," or "it."

Audiences don't want to hear about a topic, they want to experience it for themselves. If the student example at the beginning
of this chapter began by telling the audience that she was going
to talk about tools, she probably would have lost them from the
start. But she spoke to her audience. Instead of saying "I am going to talk to you about three types of tools today," she said, with
great enthusiasm, "Listen up . . . I will teach you how to use a tool
and how to use it properly and safely." We knew right away that
we were going to have an experience with tools.

4. *Make Them Laugh.* Humor is an effective way of getting the
audience's attention . . . if you're funny. If you know that you're
not funny, don't attempt humor as a way of capturing attention.
It is sure to backfire on you! However, if you can tell a joke or a
humorous story comfortably and without having to read it, it can
relax both you and the audience. You want to make sure, however, the joke or story is not contrived. Humor in a speech should
almost always connect easily to your subject. Otherwise, the au-

dience may listen to you with suspicion, wondering what sort of iron fist is hiding underneath your velvet glove! The humorous personal story in the following example works well for a speech on the subject of grief and loss.

> *My friend has a 12-year-old daughter, Emily, whose cat, Mittens, recently died on a Sunday afternoon. She was terribly upset. That evening the formal grieving process began with a little burial service for the cat in the back yard. Although Emily didn't sleep very well that night, she still managed to get up in the morning and mope off to school. In the afternoon, when she got off the bus with her best friend, she came racing around to the backyard where her father was doing some gardening. "Dad, Dad," she squeaked with excitement, "Can we get a rabbit?" Her father, being a very good parent and not wanting to deal with a rabbit (or rabbits!) in the house, responded by saying, "Sweetie, Mittens just died. You can't get over her death just by buying a new pet. You need time to let go. You need time to grieve." Without skipping a beat, Emily looked indignantly at her father and chortled, "Dad, I'm twelve years old! I grieve quickly!"*

5. Tell a Personal Story. "A funny thing happened on the way to speech class . . . ." One of the most effective ways of gaining your audience's attention is by relating a personal story or experience that connects to the subject. If the story is meaningful to you, it will likely be meaningful to your audience, as well. The following example works well for a speech on the power of the media. It uses a rhetorical question and a personal narrative:

> *Where were you? Where were you when you first heard the horrific news of September 11, 2001? I was at my desk. It was a day just like any other for me: sort through some papers; put a refill in my pen; organize my 'Things to Do Today' list. Then the phone rang. The voice at the other end of the line was shaky. She anxiously asked me, "Have you heard about the tragedy?" Having no idea of what she was talking about, I simply responded by ask-*

ing, "What tragedy?" She said four simple words: "Turn on your television!" Like many Americans, it was days before I turned it off . . .

6. *Keep Them Guessing*. In a speech, you don't always have to give away the ending in the first sentence. You can craft your words in a suspenseful way that audiences will be wondering just what you are up to as in this example from a persuasive speech on lowering the drinking age:

"I live in Baudette, Minnesota. A city located on the U.S./Canadian border. I am 19 years old. There are two bars here. One on the U.S. side of the border. The other, on the Canadian side. Right now, I am standing on the U.S. side and I want to go into the bar to have a beer, but I can't. (student takes an exaggerated step as if crossing an imaginary line) Now I am in Canada. Here, I can get into the bar and have my beer. (student steps back to U.S. side of the imaginary line) Can't have a beer. (steps back to Canadian side) Can have a beer. Does this make any sense to you? Did some unexplained phenomenon happen to me by moving my body two feet across an arbitrary line? I am nineteen years old. I can go to war and die for my country. I can get married. Raise a family. I can even purchase a house that I can return to after voting for the President of the United States of America. But I cannot open my fridge and legally pop open a beer. It doesn't make sense. Friends, I propose it is time we lowered the legal drinking age . . ." (Adapted from Brian Millard's persuasive speech on lowering the legal drinking age, —Savannah College of Art and Design)

7. *Start with a Great Quote, Fact or Statistic*. Familiar quotes are a great way to start a speech. A well-chosen quote can create quite an impact as well as orient your audience to your topic. Remember, however, that some quotes tend to sound fuzzy to your audience, especially long quotes. Don't start a speech with a poem or a long or unfamiliar quote. While it may have impacted you when you read it, for a number of reasons, it won't have the same impact with your audience. My personal rule when using a quote in an introduction is to choose a quote that is short and familiar or can be paraphrased to sound short and familiar.

Facts and statistics can have a similar impact. Some numbers may surprise your audience. Michael Moore did this in his film, *Bowling for Columbine*, which compared the rate of death by gun in the United States to that of other western countries. He showed that while some countries have as many guns, such as in Canada, the murder rate by gun was a tenth of what it is in the United States. Those numbers were powerfully striking to the audience even when they are adjusted to per capita rates.

Just be careful not to overwhelm your audience with too many numbers. You may even want to round off large numbers and talk in approximations rather than precise details. And, as always, if you are using a fact or statistic, make sure you cite the source of your information.

Here is an introduction to a speech on the subject of Factory Farming that makes use of both a great quote and some interesting facts:

> *"The non-violent, peacemaking-revolutionary, Mahatma Gandhi once said that, "the greatness of a nation and its moral progress can be judged by the way its animals are treated." How do you think the world would judge America today? - America, a nation whose family farms are rapidly being devoured by corporate, industry-modeled, farms. A country, according to Grace Factory Farm project, where many animals used for meat production never see the light of day, breathe fresh air or have the room to move about freely. I want to talk to you about factory farming today. And when I am finished, I am going to let you to be the judge . . . ."*

8. Surprise Your Audience. It would be great if every time we had to give a speech the audience members were already sitting on the edge of their seats, eager with anticipation, longing to hear what we had to say. Unfortunately, too many dull speeches have driven our audiences into a kind of low-expectation mode when it comes to speeches. This phenomenon, however, provides us the perfect opportunity to catch our audiences off guard with something surprising or startling. No one will be expecting it!

I have had a number of students who have done brave and daring stunts to capture audience attention. One student began his speech by flailing himself into the podium and then falling on the floor. We thought he was having a seizure. He delivered an excellent speech that challenged us to take ourselves less seriously. Another student entered the room wearing sunglasses, a fake moustache and a pair of boxer shorts with two well-rounded plastic buttocks sticking out from behind. He delivered a humorous, but well written, acceptance speech for the self-awarded: Buns of the Year Award.

One bright student from the Savannah Technical College began her powerful speech on child poverty by placing her forefinger in front of her lips and gently hushing the audience:

"Shhhhh! Shhhhh! I want you to listen today. But not with your ears. I want you to listen with your hearts . . . ."

Not only did she develop this powerful introduction to an equally powerful speech but also she went on to deliver the same speech to then-Governor of Georgia, Roy Barnes, and a focus group working to eradicate poverty in Georgia. Sometimes a whisper is louder than a shout!

9. Use an Audio or Visual Aid. Audio and visual aids can help a speech introduction greatly if used correctly. Remember, the aid in the introduction is being used to capture attention at this point and nothing else. You don't want to use a visual aid in an introduction to launch into too much information. To make it effective, keep it simple. Like the young man who began his speech on Motorcycle Helmets by entering the room to the sound of fast rock music, wearing a motorcycle helmet and holding a photo of a badly injured human head in his hands. He didn't say anything

Bonus Track
The two most important parts of a speech that should be delivered without any notes at all: the introduction and conclusion. The introduction, because you want to use eye contact to help establish your credibility from the outset and the conclusion, because you want to tell your audience that you sincerely believe what you have just told them. Reading at either of these points can destroy even a great speech!

at first. He simply walked up and down the aisles showing people the grotesque image. As the disgusting photo neared each person, three simple words underneath the image could be read: *Wear a Helmet!*

Three Rules for Audio or Visual Aids

If you are going to use some sort of audio-visual bear in mind three important guidelines:

1. Keep It Short—You don't want your A/V to overshadow your speech.
2. Make Sure It Is Cued and Ready to Go. Nothing cools off an audience or embarrasses a speaker more than a speech that begins with awkward technical difficulties.
3. Make Sure You Can Still Deliver Your Speech Even If Your Audio or Visual Aid Doesn't Work—remember Murphy's Law: Anything that can, will go wrong!

Establish Your Credibility

Sometime around the late six century B.C., the early Greek philosopher, Heraclitus, said that, "Character is destiny." In other words, where we will be tomorrow depends on who we are today. The same can be said of a speech. Where a speech goes depends upon how it begins. Our personal character at the beginning of a speech, in many ways, will determine how it concludes. In the introduction of a speech, you have the opportunity to show your audience that you are trustworthy and likeable.

You may want to do a quick review of chapter three, Developing Your Personal Credibility, at this point. Here, I will highlight five particular ways to strengthen your ethos in an introduction.

Five Effective Ways to Establish Your Credibility

1. Make Eye Contact. There is not a more important time in a speech to make eye contact than in the introduction. The eyes are the window to the soul. This is the time for your eyes to tell your audience that your soul is trustworthy, confident and competent.

If you can learn the introduction to your speech well enough not to need notes, it will be all the better. Look members of your audience in their eyes and tell them that you respect them enough not to be hiding behind your notes. If you are still too nervous to look them in the eyes, look them in the forehead!

2. Smile. When you smile at your audience, you send out a variety of messages, such as: you are glad to be there; you are enthusiastic about your message; what you have to say is going to be good; you are likeable; you like your audience and you like being with them today; you have confidence in yourself and competence in your subject. A smile has the power to inspire a positive mood change in both you and your audience. Smile and the whole world will smile with you. So make sure you brush that piece of spinach out of your teeth and at the beginning of your speech, give your audience an authentic, whitest and brightest, smile.

3. Laugh at Yourself. I have a friend, a prominent psychologist, who had been invited to address a small country church just a few weeks after he had gotten his degree from graduate school. He was overly sure of himself and puffed up with pride. When he arrived at the speaking engagement he was overwhelmed at the sight of all the cars that had swelled the parking lot and were streaming up and down the roadside for quite some distance. "All these people have come to hear me speak today. Wow, I must be pretty hot stuff," he mused to himself.

When it was time to speak the country church was filled to capacity accept for a few empty spots in the old pews up near the front.

My friend was stepping up to the pulpit when noticed a few women near the back of the room standing—large women, fanning themselves in the warm foyer. "Too hot to stand and listen to the great psychologist," he thought. In his arrogance he stopped his speech, singled out the women and waved them to the front: "Ladies, please come down to the front. There are a few spaces up here."

He felt fully in command of the situation until he heard a

mouthful of embarrassing words come flooding forth from his lips as the women sat down in the old pews: "And ladies, mind the cracks in your seats."

He gasped. The audience gasped. For a split second, that felt to my friend an eternity, the room was silent. And then all at once everyone in the audience broke into uproarious laughter. My friend felt his face grow hot with embarrassment. It took every ounce of humility to regain his composure and salvage his speech. He told me that from that day forth, he would begin to take himself far less seriously.

If something goes wrong at the beginning of your speech, and quite often something does—a video player doesn't work or instead of greeting your audience with eloquent words of thanks, your head erupts with a volcanic sneeze - be willing to laugh at yourself. Lighten-up! It can change the mood of your whole speech in a positive and friendly way. When we take ourselves too seriously, our audience takes us less seriously. Nothing exemplifies humility more than an ability to laugh at ourselves, especially when something is obviously funny.

At the same time, you don't need to be self-deprecating. Speakers who put themselves down in an attempt to be funny or to deflect their own insecurity will make the audience feel uncomfortable. For example, making a joke about your apparent weight problem is not a good way to begin a speech about body image.

Just relax and go with the flow. If something is obviously funny, don't be afraid to laugh.

4. Speak from Verifiable Knowledge. The introduction is your opportunity to show the audience that you have researched your subject and that, although you may not be an expert in the field, you have studied what the experts have to say. You instill trust in your audience by showing them that you are not simply talking about personal knowledge on a subject, but accountable knowledge—knowledge that can be verified. For example, if you are giving a speech on the sport of soccer, you can tell your audience your opinion that you think it is a great sport but also let them know that there is verifiable evidence to support your opinion, as in the following speech:

> *I want to talk to today about a sport that strengthens me phys-*
> *ically, mentally and even spirtually. A sport that I began play-*
> *ing at the age of four and still play today. It's a sport that I*
> *have enjoyed playing casually with friends on a sunny Sat-*
> *urday morning and competively in the cold and in the rain.*
> *But don't let that scare you. It is a sport that just about any-*
> *one can play. It is a great sport and it's popularity is sweep-*
> *ing the nation. In the 1980s, The President's Council on Phys-*
> *ical Fitness and Sport called it the fastest growing high school*
> *sport in United States. And the book,* Cultural Dimensions
> of Play, Games and Sport *referred to it as a "cultural phe-*
> *nomenon" in America. What sport am I talking about? Soc-*
> *cer—according to the* U.S Soccer on-line, *the fastest growing*
> *amateur sport in America.*

*5. **Speak from Personal Knowledge**.* Whereas, verifiable
knowledge intills trust in our audience, personal knowledge in-
stills friendliness and receptivity. Personal knowledge creates a
personal three-way connection between us, our audience and our
subject. It tells the audience why we are even bothering to talk
about this particular subject at all. It shows them that the subject is
important to us and , therefore, will likely be interesting to them.
A good introduction will build the speaker's credibilty by having
a good balance of both verfiable knowledge and personal knowledge as in the example in number four above.

Preview Your Message.

How frustrating it would be to be a passenger on a trip without
knowing what your destination was or how you were going to get
there. Unless we had signed on for a mystery tour, we'd probably
grow weary half way through and ask for our money back. By
previewng your message, you reveal both the general destination
of your speech and your means of getting there.

As mentioned previously, however, it doesn't mean you have

to lay the whole plan out in specific detail. Previewing your message in the introduction simply lets your audience know that you have a plan and that you are willing to reveal a little of that plan to them.

Previewing your message for your audience is not only a helpful and friendly thing to do, it is critical to the success of your speech! Remember, at least in general terms, Tell them what you are going to tell them! And then tell them how. It will help them get ready mentally for what is to follow.

In the example we used at the very beginning of this chapter, the student clearly revealed both her destination and her means of getting us there. Her destination was to teach us how to use tools safely and effectively. And her means of getting us to that destination was by way of a topically designed speech: drill, hammer and screwdriver. By previewing your message, you let your audience in on the plan. You tell them what you are going to tell them. And you tell them how.

Conclusions

Many potentially great speeches have been ineffective simply because the speaker failed to imagine a creative way to end the speech. Too often speakers find themselves verbally rambling around in front of the audience in search of the right words with which to conclude. Without a well-formulated conclusion, speakers often end their speeches with awkward words like: "Well that's about it." Or, "I guess I am done." Or, by using the infamous words of Porky the Pig: "That's all, folks!"

At its simplest level, a conclusion puts the brakes on the speech. It is the kind and generous act of telling your audience that the speech is over and that they are free to offer their applause if they so choose.

But an effective conclusion does much more than stop the motion of the speech. An effective conclusion is your opportunity to thank the audience, to remind them of what you have just told them and to tell your audience why your subject is important or how it can be helpful for them. In some cases, particularly when it comes to persuasive speaking, a good conclusion will also give the audience some clear direction on a particular action you are persuading them to take.

A good conclusion doesn't happen by accident. It needs to be intentional, well planned and imaginative. It also needs to be simple and concise. Here are five time-tested, powerful methods you might use to end your speech.

Five Powerful Ways to End a Speech

1. *Say Thank You.* To say thank you to the audience may not be the most powerful way of ending a speech, in fact, it may not be powerful at all, but it is simple and it is effective. And besides, it sounds a whole lot better to the audience than listening to you fumble around trying to dig your way out of your speech. Two words: Thank you.

2. *Echo the Introduction.* One of the most common and effective ways of ending the speech is to echo the introduction. You don't need to quote your introduction verbatim. That's not the point. The idea here is to tie your speech together by connecting your conclusion back to your introduction by using some of the same words, restating a quote, or connecting us back to a story you used in your introduction. The following example dealing with grief and loss concludes the speech that was introduced above (see example of an introduction under subheading, 4 *Make Them Laugh*):

> *So even if you are like 12 year old Emily and you grieve quickly, I am sure by now you can see that grieving is still important and something not to be rushed. Nobody likes loss but when it comes our way it is reassuring to know that we're not alone. Just be open to it, patient with it, and embracing of it. The grieving process has much to teach us. Thank you.*

3. *Ask a Rhetorical Question.* In some cases, the best way to conclude a speech is to ask a rhetorical question. In a conclusion, a rhetorical question assumes that everyone will have the same an-

swer based on the contents of the speech and so is asked less for a response and more for effect, like the student who gave a tribute speech to honor his brother. In his speech, he told his audience the story of how his brother used to motivate him in childhood by asking him, "Are you ready to rock?" His brother even got him to go bungee jumping and when he almost chickened-out, his brother whispered in his ear, "Are you ready to rock?" And he jumped with inspiration and courage. He ended his speech, by asking the class that same question: "Are you ready to rock?"

One speech on the subject of exercise ended with a series of options followed by a rhetorical question:

I suppose we could idly waste away the rest of our lives basking in the blue glow of our television screens, or slowly ooze into an emotional funk and possibly depression due to physical inactivity. Nobody is forcing us to get active, to get healthy, or to feel great. It's just a choice that we get to make. Feel bad or feel good. It's that simple. Which do you choose? Thank you.

4. ***End with a Story.*** One way to give your speech more impact is to conclude with a brief story that brings home the ideas contained in your speech. Narratives have a powerful ability to communicate ideas and emotions. They reach the audience at a much deeper level than facts or statistics. Not only can a story tie together your ideas neatly, ending with a story can be a dramatic way of making your audience sympathetic to your view point as in the following example on the subject of the effects of smoking:

I have been talking to you today about the harmful effects of smoking cigarettes. People who smoke get sick more often, have a higher risk for heart disease and strokes, and increase their chances of getting cancer by 60%. There is a very high price to pay for those who smoke and even those who don't. My father is 55 years old. He has smoked cigarettes everyday for 40 years. He is still alive today. Not always healthy, but alive. Up until last year you couldn't argue with him. He always said, "It's my life, it's my choice." But last year, my mother, a non-smoker was diagnosed with lung cancer. "How can it be?" she asked her doctor. She told my mother that her risk of cancer was just as high, if not higher, because she lived with a smoker. Today, my father is trying to come to terms with the fact that whenever he lit up a cigarette, not only did he put himself at risk, he put the love of his life in grave jeopardy. If you can't quit for yourself, then maybe you can quit for the one you love. Thank you.

5. ***End with a Quote.*** Ending with a quote can be effective by creating a sense of closure for your speech and your audience. Quotes work best when they are not too long or too formal. Ending with poem or lengthy passage used to be a quite popular technique among orators even as recent as twenty or thirty years ago. It is not nearly as effective today. The general rule with quotes in conclusions today is the same as it is for quotes in introductions: short and familiar as in the example below:

> *I believe the best way to deal with any life-threatening disease is to stay positive. I also greatly respect anyone who is dealing with that kind of challenge. It really makes you stop and appreciate the finer details in life, the sorts of things so many of us usually take for granted, like holding a pen or walking up a flight of stairs. So don't look upon the physically challenged with pity, instead focus on the amazing strength and courage of these survivors. And remember the saying, "Experience is not what happens to a man, it is what a man does with what happens to him." Thank you.* (Adapted from Sara Cohen's speech on scleroderma, Savannah College of Art and Design.)

And In Conclusion

If our conclusions are imaginative and well crafted in simple and concise ways, we should never have to say, "And in conclusion," or similar words. Our audiences will know that we are coming to a close. Use your closing remarks wisely so that you may take advantage of your final opportunity to thank the audience, to remind them of what you have just told them and to tell them why the subject is important or how it can be helpful for them.

How Long Should My Introduction and Conclusion Be?

Try not to get too stressed-out by rigid rules about time lengths for introductions and conclusions. Generally speaking, however, the time length of an introduction and conclusion should total no more than one fifth of the total length of the speech. For example, a five-minute speech should allow about one minute total for both the introduction and conclusion: roughly thirty seconds to introduce the speech and thirty seconds to conclude it. The most important thing to remember, however, is that you don't let your introduction or conclusion consume too much of your allotted time. For example, don't use up so much time telling a long story, no matter how good it is, in the introduction that you are unable to treat your subject thoroughly.

Upon Reflection

1. What is your life's most embarrassing moment? Are you still sensitive about it or can you laugh at yourself?
2. Make two lists pertaining to the subject of reading. The first list should contain personal knowledge about the subject. The second should contain verifiable knowledge.
3. What is your favorite quote? Why?
4. Write a paragraph or two describing the impact of AIDS on our culture using facts and statistics. Make sure to cite your sources.
5. Now write a paragraph or two on the impact of AIDS on our culture using a brief narrative or personal story.

— 11 —

Researching

If you think education is costly, try ignorance!

IF YOU WANT TO sound like a pro then sound like you know! Speeches that are simply opinion-based musings or personal, experience-centered reflections may be slightly entertaining but are hardly efficacious in teaching or persuading unless they are fortified with verifiable knowledge. Opinions, personal knowledge and the like are best when strengthened by the complement of well-earned research.

Jenkin Lloyd Jones, the early twentieth century child labor opponent and trade union supporter once said that, "A speech is a solemn responsibility. The man who makes a bad thirty-minute speech to two hundred people wastes only a half hour of his own time. But he wastes one hundred hours of the audience's time - more than four days—which should be a hanging offense." Speakers whose words are based solely on opinion or whose entire source of information is their own personal experience are not only unethical and undisciplined, they waste the audience's time. Be warned and be careful! In some states it soon may be a hanging offense!

Although when it comes to giving a speech, a good place to begin is with a topic for which we already have some personal knowledge, that personal knowledge must lead us to further study and deeper understanding. For example, if you have been taking horseback riding lessons for five months, it might seem like a good idea for you to give a speech that informs your audi-

> Verifiable knowledge is knowledge of a particular subject that can be proven, supported, demonstrated and/or confirmed in some way other than our own experience of it.

ence about riding. But your own personal knowledge, in and of itself, is not sufficient for a speech that teaches or informs. The world of riding is thousands of times bigger than your own experience. You need to be able to make references to what the experts in the field have to say about the subject, the facts and the statistics. By using verifiable knowledge, you are saying to your audience that you understand that, although you have some very good personal experience with riding, your smaller experience is really just reflective of a larger body of knowledge.

We need to go to that larger body of knowledge and glean from it verifiable evidence which supports our teaching or our position. Verifiable knowledge is knowledge that can be proven, supported, demonstrated and/or confirmed in some way other than our own experience of it. Great speechwriters know the importance of drawing out information from that larger body of knowledge and how to use it as support evidence for their subjects.

Personal experience can be the jumping-off place or impetus for your speech. But verifiable knowledge must be used not only to augment your own personal knowledge but also to validate it. Moreover, when we do a thorough job with research, we find that our own ideas and opinions tend get reshaped or grow in new directions. Like a tree bending toward the light, our hungry minds tend to grow toward truth if it is available.

The teacher/poet, Taylor Mali has written a moving piece called Like Lilly Like Wilson, about a recovering "like" addict who sets out to write a paper on why homosexuals shouldn't be allowed to adopt children. However, she has a hard time finding resources, "which is to say, ones that back her up." She says that all her research argues "in favor of what I thought I was against." Her mind is changed by her research and she decides to write a paper making the exact opposite claim that, homosexuals should be allowed to adopt children. It's the research that has done it for her.

As we mature, we learn that the blessings of writing and giving speeches are not that we get to share our opinions or ideas, but that by engaging in the activity of speech writing and giving speeches, we learn who we are and where we stand on topics and issues. The process should open up to us the many and wonderful shades and illusive nuances of our overwhelming and mysterious world, and take us to deeper understanding. We may start with a hypothesis, but quite often, when we set out to do our research and then engage in the struggle and pain of putting our feelings down in words, we discover, like Lilly Wilson, that we have been moved to a new place in our thinking. In other words, sometimes we give speeches not because we already understand, but in order to understand.

Taylor Mali moves toward the end of his Like Lilly poem by saying that, "changing your mind is one of the best ways of finding out whether or not you still have one. Or even that minds are like parachutes, that it doesn't matter what you pack them with so long as they open at the right time." Keep your mind open, do the research and you will discover some pretty amazing things about yourself and others and the amazing world in which you live.

Good Sources of Verifiable Knowledge

www.Internet. There are many places we can turn when looking for verifiable knowledge. Probably the most accessible source of information is the Internet. In fact, in a recent article in the New York Times, Thomas Friedman reports that the "Google" search engine processes approximately 200 million searches per day! (T. Friedman, "Is Google God," *New York Times*, June 29, 2003). The World Wide Web also offers the advantage of getting your news from sources around the world. Sometimes it is helpful to get a perspective on world events from countries other than your own. Two of my favorites are CBC.ca/world (Canada) and ith.com (the International Herald Tribune. But accessible source does not necessarily mean good source. There are certain factors that you will want to be aware of if you are going to surf the precarious seas of the World Wide Web in search of solid material for your speech:

> Whereas verifiable knowledge instills trust in our audience, personal knowledge instills friendliness and receptivity.

- Does the website offer an e-mail address which you can use to verify the evidence on the page?

- Does the website offer citations or make references to the source of its information?
- As with any article found in any other source, are the author's name, credentials or professional affiliations listed?
- Is the material relevant or timely? It is unethical, not to mention just plain careless, to use outdated research material. It can also be quite embarrassing if your audience is familiar with more recent research than yours.
- Who is the publisher of the website in question? Is it Billy-Bob's Gator Huntin' page or is it FloridaStateUniversity.edu? Some websites offer lots of flash and style, but very litle in the way of substance. Don't get fooled by bells and whistles.

"When I get a little money I buy books; and if any is left, I buy food and clothing. "—Desiderius Erasmus

2. Books. Books may not be as easily accessible in the cyber age as information found on the Internet but they currently have an advantage over the information highway in that they are not usually rushed. Authors have spent time laboring for truth and knowledge and, if you are willing to labor with them, their research and their writings will yield up a wisdom that cannot be grasped in a pop-up page, in Microsoft Encarta or even in Wikipedia! Books also chase down knowledge at a deeper level—knowledge that is more than "ten minutes ago!"

3. Journals and Magazines. Journals tend to be scholarly and audience specific, usually written for professionals in a particular field. Magazines, while still knowledgeable, tend to be simpler and written for a wider audience. Both journals and magazines can be helpful tools in speech writing. Although not a replacement for books or the Internet, they are a good compromise between the two. They usually offer more in-depth research than many of the pages you will find on the Internet, and yet, are timelier than many books.

4. Newscasts. Newscasts are helpful in speech preparation too. Some are more helpful than others and have a reputation for offering more journalistic integrity than sensational flash and sizzle. Get to know which ones are known for thorough and responsible research. And, as always, make sure to cite your source.

5. *Interviews.* Whether personal or professional, interviews are an excellent way of fortifying your speech with verifiable knowledge. Interviews are especially helpful when you are looking for either the testimony of an expert in the field or a narrative from someone who has personal experience with a subject.

The Source Citing Advantage.

Can we really trust knowledge that cannot be verified? Knowledge that isn't verifiable is no better than hearsay. At best it is secondhand. Using knowledge that cannot be verified is misleading and unethical. It teaches audiences to be distrustful and unhealthily cynical. Not to mention, if we are caught using information that cannot be verified, it is an embarrassment to us. President George W. Bush got caught using information which could not be verified in his January 28th, 2003 State of the Union Address. It was an embarrassment for him, his administration, and the United States of America. Don't let that happen to you!

> Beware of false knowledge; it is more dangerous than ignorance.
> —*George Bernard Shaw*

When you state a fact or cite a statistic, tell your audience where the information came from. A citation answers the questions: Who said it? Where was the research done? When and where was the particular piece of information published? If you can answer one or two of these questions when you share your information, it will lend more credence to what you are saying. You don't need to give every small detail about the source in the body of your speech, copyright date, page number, etc., but you should be able to provide it if afterwards you are questioned.

Compare the following two examples from speeches concerned with drunk driving:

Example One:

More and more, every time you go out for a drive, it seems like someone is crossing a line or weaving uncontrollably back and forth causing dangers to everyone else on the road. There are approximately 17,000 drunk driving fatalities each year. In fact, a lot of the accidents on our roads and highways are due to alcohol.

Example Two:

More and more, every time you go out for a drive, it seems like someone is crossing a line or weaving uncontrollably back and forth causing dangers to everyone else on the road. According to the National Highway Traffic Safety Administration (NHTSA), in the year 2002, there were over 17,000 drunk-driving fatalities in the United States. In fact, almost half of the deaths on America's highways and byways are alcohol related. The NHTSA reported that of the 42,815 traffic fatalities 17,419 of them involved alcohol. That's 41 percent. 41 percent of all deaths on our roads have one common denominator: alcohol.

Notice in the first example, the speech has not verified the statistic concerning the number of alcohol related traffic fatalities. It doesn't say where the source of information is coming from and, therefore, leaves us wondering if what the speaker is saying really has any credibility or if the speaker him or herself has any credibility (don't forget Ethos!). Maybe the speaker made up the statistics just to endorse a personal opinion or gut feeling, or maybe the speaker heard the number 17,000 somewhere along the line but was too lazy to go and find out where it came from. Moreover, the speaker has misquoted the second statistic by saying "In fact, a lot of the accidents on our roads and highways are due to alcohol." The actual statistics, provided by the National Highway Traffic Safety Administration refers to fatalities not accidents.

The second example is much stronger. By stating the source of the information, the speaker has left little doubt as to the validity of the statement and, therefore, has strengthened the credibility of the statement and his or her own personal credibility. This speaker has also identified the year and place to which the statistics refer. Time: the year 2002. Place: the United States of America.

Good research and proper citations will fortify your speeches and make you a much more credible and ethical speaker. If you want to sound like a pro, sound like you know!

Upon Reflection

1. Try to find three different types of resources (one book, one Internet, one journal or interview, etc.) for the subject of Sleep Deficiency in America.

2. Make an appointment with someone who was born before 1950, develop a list of questions and interview them concerning their personal experience regarding the Vietnam War?

3. Watch two different newscasts on the same day—one local station and one national. How were similar stories reported?

4. Visit the following web sources for news:
   - http://www.msnbc.msn.com (U.S.)
   - http://www.pbs.org/newshour (U.S. Public)
   - http://news.bbc.co.uk/ (British Broadcasting)
   - http://www.cbc.ca/ (Canadian Broadcasting).

   What are the top or feature stories? Is there a difference in the reporting style? Is there a different emphasis within similar stories?

— 12 —

Finding the Right Topic

Now if it's more than a new pair of jeans, some pocket money
and a place to go, Then we better get up and scream at the top
of our lungs like it was gonna die if we didn't make it so!
—Something Wild, *John Hiatt*

WHAT IS IMPORTANT TO you? What things would die if you didn't get up and scream them out at the top of your lungs or at least say them aloud? I am sure somewhere on your list, you would include things like love or truth or knowledge. Or maybe you would include your dreams and aspirations or beliefs and values. In some ways, it would be easy for public speakers if they were always given a topic on which they might speak. But sometimes we are left on our own to decide what is important enough to us to develop into a full-blown speech.

As a preacher, I have to develop a twenty to thirty minute speech every week. In my faith tradition it is called a sermon. Someone once joked that Sundays come at a preacher like telephone poles along the highway! As you can imagine, every now and then, the well of creativity seems to run dry.

It is in those times, the times when I am struggling to figure out just what on earth I should be talking about, that I tend go back to three very basic questions. What excites me? What angers me? And what makes me curious? Somewhere within the answer to one of these questions is the seed of my topic. In my mind I shake those questions like a tree and wait to see if any fruit falls to the ground. If some fruit does happen to drop, I kick it around for a bit, turn it over and over, look at it from a variety of angles to see if a seed of a topic is beginning to emerge. It may take a day or two of shaking but if I can be patient with the process, a topic usually begins to germinate in my mind.

What Excites You?

Often times the most enjoyable speeches are motivated by the speaker's own excitement about the subject. The audience can see the excitement in the speaker's enthusiastic smile, or feel it radiating from his or her energy or conviction about the subject.

I recently heard a great speech comparing Electro-Static audio speakers to Electro-Magnetic audio speakers. To some, that topic may have sounded as dull as a dreary day in Duluth! But to this particular audiophile the subject was the nexus of his own excitement, his prior interest and knowledge in the subject, and the challenging task at hand —giving a speech to a group of college students. And it made for a wonderfully entertaining and informative presentation.

Some previous speeches that have been given because speakers were excited about a topic included:

- Flirting
- Snow Boarding
- Analogue sound verses digital sound
- The Volkswagen Beetle
- Juggling
- Favorite Cities
- Favorite Musicians and Artists
- Video Gaming
- Quakers

If you are searching for a topic, sit down with a piece of paper and a pen and brainstorm a list of things that excite you.

What Angers You?

Some of the most passionate speeches are inspired by an agitation about a particular issue, event or even a particular person, such as a world leader or local politician. Maybe you are frustrated by something or someone. Perhaps, you are restless for change. These are great places to begin developing a speech.

The answer to the question, What Angers You?, often leads to exciting and altruistic speeches which are delivered with passion and conviction. What rubs you the wrong way? Here is a list of some of the things others have been angered by enough to speak about!

- Child Hunger
- Poverty
- Gay and Lesbian Rights
- The Cost of Education
- The Cutting of Music and Arts from Education
- Homelessness
- SPAM
- The War in Iraq
- Presidential Policies or Practices
- Meat Production/Factory Farming
- Animal Rights
- Fur
- Body Image in the Media

What Makes You Curious?

Curiosity may have killed the cat, but it also has made for some excellent speeches! If we are curious about a particular subject, chances are, others will be too. And not only will our curiosity create interest for us, it will create interest for others. I have seen audiences glued to a speaker simply because the speaker chose to answer a question we all were a little curious about.

For example, I once had a student who gave a demonstration speech on how a television works. Most Americans watch a little television everyday, usually more than we will admit, but very few of us know how the thing works. Another student chose to give a speech on Freudian Slips. Like most of us, she had heard the term, Freudian slip, before, but that was about the extent of it. So her curiosity led her on a quest to know more. In the end she developed an excellent informative speech with three categories: slips of the tongue, slips of action and slips memory.

Other speeches whose impetus was curiosity include:

- How to make Thai Satay Chicken.
- How to live well on a shoestring.
- How did the President really become President?
- Giving Blood (this student's curiosity actually led her to give blood for the first time!).
- What is in our fast food?
- What does "organic" mean?
- What a person needs to know to enjoy the history of Savannah, Georgia

But Will It Work?

Once you have narrowed down a topic, there are a few other questions you will want to ask yourself before deciding if this particular subject is a good topic to develop into a speech.

Can I Access Verifiable Knowledge on the Subject? You may be excited about a topic, or be angry or curious about something, but you need to ask yourself if there is information about that particular subject available and if you can access that information. As you will remember from our last chapter, verifiable knowledge is knowledge of a particular subject that can be proven, supported, demonstrated and/or confirmed in some way other than our own experience of it.

In some cases, the problem will be that there is not enough information on a particular subject easily available. In other cases, particularly if you haven't narrowed your subject sufficiently, there will be too much information.

Can My Speech Be Delivered in the Time Allotted? Am I going to be able to do a thorough job with this topic in the time that I have to speak? Maybe the topic is too extensive or too broad. You may need to rethink the subject or narrow it some more.

Have I Narrowed the Topic Sufficiently? Sometimes speakers come up with a great speech topic but it is too broad a topic. Make sure you are not trying to bite off more than you or the audience can chew! In this case, try to focus on only one aspect of the subject. For example, a topic like "snowboarding" is broad. A speech dealing with this subject could be quite lengthy if all aspects of snowboarding were treated thoroughly and responsibly. You would need to include topics such as: "how to snowboard," the "history of snowboarding," "equipment needed," "amateur and pro snowboarding," "Olympic snowboarding," etc. If you have only a short period of time, it would be best to pick just one aspect, such as the History of Snowboarding.

Who Cares? As mentioned above, if you are enthusiastic about your subject, chances are your audience will be too! But if you have just picked something out of the blue in order to have something to talk about, you are in for a cold response from the audience. The best topics—the ones which will involve the audience - involve you too!

Upon Reflection

1. What or who excites you? Why?
2. Develop a short and imaginative speech that informs people about your favorite musician.
3. What rubs you the wrong way? Why?
4. With some friends or student colleagues develop a talk show dealing with a controversial issue.
5. What makes you curious? Why not try and figure it out today!
6. Develop a short and interesting presentation that demonstrates how modern plumbing works.

—13 —

The Persuasive Speech

I would rather try to persuade a man to go along,
because once I have persuaded him he will stick. If I scare him,
he will stay just as long as he is scared, and then he is gone.
—Dwight D. Eisenhower

MENTION THE WORD "PERSUADE" and people get nervous. We know something is going to be asked of us and so we put ourselves on guard, level orange alert, protecting ourselves from being duped once again.

Mention the word "persuade" and a wave of images washes over us. Most of these are negative: a slick lawyer convincing a jury that his unscrupulous client is not guilty; a smooth talking, perfectly quaffed televangelist tricking the sick and elderly out of their monthly social security checks; an infomercial promising perfect abs, buns of steel or rapid weight loss if we will just purchase yet another useless fitness gadget which will likely sit in the closet collecting dust as we continue making those low monthly payments; a dozen spammed commercials in our inbox page or a mealtime telephone call from a telemarketer who swears up and down that they are not trying to sell anything, they are just "taking a survey."

I hear the word "persuasion" and I think of the time, many years ago, when my oldest brother persuaded me to sit on an anthill full of red ants for ten minutes in order to join his neighborhood spy club. No wonder we're nervous. Mention the word persuade, and we get stressed.

Manipulation

But maybe what we are talking about here is not persuasion at all, but manipulation. The term, "manipulation," comes from the Latin word manipulus that literally translated means "handful." At the root of manipulus, though, is another Latin word, manus, which means "hand." Manipulation and underhanded are similar words both in root and meaning. They have a negative connotation. To manipulate someone or something really means to handle them or manually (another 'manus' word) arrange things! In a colloquial sense, we might say a manipulator underhandedly "plays" his or her audience by "fixing" knowledge and/or the situation. Manipulation is deceptive. It is a trick. That's why we often say, "the hand is quicker than the eye!"

In her fine book, *The Story Factor: Inspiration, Influence, and Persuasion through the Art of Story Telling*, Annette Simmons has come up with a great definition for manipulation. Simmons says that manipulation is the act of "getting people to believe a story that isn't quite true." Since the story (or information) will not convince people on its own merits (after all it's not true), the speaker is required to manually coerce the information to get the audience to accept it. As you can imagine, it takes a great deal of effort to convince someone to accept a story that isn't quite true. Dwight D. Eisenhower once put it this way, "I would rather try to persuade a man to go along, because once I have persuaded him he will stick. If I scare him, he will stay just as long as he is scared, and then he is gone."

Simmons calls manipulation "an inferior method of influence" with bothersome ethics. After all, you have to hang around to keep scaring your audience into action. Besides, Simmons argues, "there is a much more powerful source of influence available to anyone with experience as a human being—telling an authentically persuasive story."

Persuasion

Persuasion comes from another Latin word *suadere*, which means to urge or advise. From *suadere* we get other English words such as "assuage" and "suave". Add the prefix, "per," which means through, all over or completely, to the verb "suādēre" and you begin to see a word that means to convince thoroughly or be convinced thoroughly. To persuade is not to manipulate an audience or even a situation, rather, to persuade is to provide the opportunity and the understanding necessary for your audience to make an informed, wise, and favorable decision. Good persuasive speakers know that they need not coerce an audience simply to advise and urge them. Persuasive speaking is also far more ethical and trustworthy than manipulation.

The Ethics of Persuasion

We will go into more details on the subject of ethics and communication later on, but for now suffice it to say that to persuade ethically a speaker needs to have a respect for both the audience and the information he or she is using:

- Respect the Audience: Don't ask your audience to do anything you wouldn't do. Remember to apply the golden rule, treat you audience in a way that you would like to be treated.
- Respect the Information: Make sure to cite your sources. Don't plagiarize or quote out of context. Be sure you are using verifiable knowledge to persuade and not false information or just a swell of emotion.

An Intrusion

Still, even when the basic ethical principles of persuasion are being applied, some people will object to it. They see persuasion as an intrusion into their lives, attitudes or decisions. They argue that unless they invite a persuasive discourse they should not be subjected to it. And to a certain degree, we can all relate to this position. After all, every one of us has experienced times when someone tried to persuade us when we really didn't want to be persuaded. We grow weary of overly zealous religious people who attempt to convert us at our own front door or telephone solicitors who interrupt an important conversation or family meal. Unwelcome persuasion is tiresome.

The Necessity of Persuasion

Still, the art of persuasion has been around for a long, long time. It is necessary to the advancement of our society. In Antidosis, Isocrates stated that "...because there has been implanted in us the power to persuade each other and to make clear to each other whatever we desire, not only have we escaped the life of wild beasts, but we have come together and founded cities and made laws and invented arts; and generally speaking, there is no institution devised by man which the power of speech has not helped us to establish." It is the art and the very act of persuasion that have helped us to evolve as a civilization.

Think about it, in many ways persuasion is what keeps us from killing each other. If we couldn't persuade each other with our words, we'd likely resort to force or violence to maintain a particular political system or power structure.

The twentieth century novelist and philosopher, Ayn Rand once said that "there are only two means by which men can deal with one another: guns or logic. Force or persuasion. Those who know that they cannot win by means of logic, have always resorted to guns." For the most part, in the United States of America, we have chosen persuasion over force. Although, we have kept a few guns around just in case!

Reaching the Goal

As mentioned previously, the act of persuading is simply to provide the opportunity and the understanding necessary for your audience to make an informed, wise, and favorable decision. That is the act of persuading. The goal of persuasive speaking, however, is to encourage your audience to think or act differently. Persuasive speech changes hearts and minds and lives.

The Process of Persuasion

In his book, *Handbook of Social Psychology*, W.J. McGuire has shown that to motivate an audience to think or act differently, a certain cognitive and emotional process within the audience must first occur. One of the greatest pitfalls persuasive speakers will walk into is rushing their audience too quickly to think or act differently without allowing this process of persuasion to evolve.

Awareness. How can our audience even think about change if they are not first aware of a need or problematic situation? If we suspect that an audience knows little about a particular subject, the first order of business, after gaining their attention, will be to make the audience aware of the issue.

Understanding. Okay, you have made your audience aware of the need or issue, but do they understand it? Do they see it as a problem or something that could or needs to be changed? At what level do they understand the issue?

Acceptance. Once an audience has been made aware of an issue and understands the issue, you then have the opportunity to persuade them to accept your position or agree with it. You may not be able to get them to act on it yet, but if you can get your audience to a place of agreement, depending on the need or situation, you will have already achieved some success. If you have only one short opportunity to address your audience, and if the issue is new to them, you may set the more realistic end of acceptance or agreement as your goal.

> Think of the mental steps in persuasion as rungs on a ladder, which begin with awareness and lead up to action.

If the audience already has prior awareness concerning an issue, for example drinking and driving, or if you have more than one opportunity to address your audience, then you might set your sights a little higher and aim for motivating your audience to take action.

Retention. If you want your audience to act, they will need to remember why they are supposed to act. In other words, part of the process of persuasion is to help your audience integrate their acceptance with their own values and behavioral patterns. For example, if you want your audience to begin recycling, you will want to plant some sort of seed (an image works well) so that the next time they are about to toss an empty bottle in the trash, they will think twice and, instead, consider placing it in a bin for recycling. They need to remember what they mentally and emotionally accepted during your speech so that they can be ready to act upon it when the time comes.

Action. The fifth and final step in the process of persuasion is, you guessed it, action. That was your goal in the first place, right? Once you have helped your audience through the first four steps in the process of persuasion, you are ready to help them act.

- *Be clear and be specific* about what you would like your audience to do. Don't simply talk in general or vague terms like, "So let's start recycling." Be precise as in the following example:

So remember, put your glass in the glass bin and your paper in the paper bin. Save the planet for your children and theirs! Blue box this week and every week!

- *Provide opportunities for your audience to act.* For example, don't just ask them to write their senator regarding an issue. Instead, bring in a sample letter, complete with self-addressed, stamped envelopes for everyone in your audience to take with them.

Remember, the process of persuasion is the mental and emotional process that your audience needs to experience if its members are going to be motivated to change the way they think or act. Let your well-crafted and imaginative words guide the audience through the steps of this necessary process.

Three Effective Designs for Persuasive Speeches
Problem-Solution. The name pretty well says it all, here. The problem-solution is a simple design that identifies problems and proposes solutions. For example, if the problem is that many of our lakes are dying. The solution might be to persuade the audience to take action to reduce the misuse of the lakes and the land surrounding the lakes.

The structure of the problem-solution speech develops points for each problem and points for each solution. For example:

Problem –Many Lakes Are Dying from:
1. Run off from paving and over-development.
2. Run-off from heavily fertilized nearby farms.

Solution—Reduce the Misuse by:
1. Allowing only perforated parking lots when new development or repaving occurs.
2. Restrict type and amount of inorganic pesticides

Each point in the Problem-Solution design is developed with the same type of point structure that is employed in informative speaking.

Point—Counter Point. Unwittingly, I first learned of the point-counter point design for persuasive speaking as a young teenager while watching the "Not Ready for Prime Time Players" on the hugely successful late night television show, *Saturday Night Live.* Each week, Jane Curtain and Dan Aykroyd would square off against one another in a formal debate over one hot issue or another in a sketch called "Point/Counter-Point." Curtain was usually the more progressive and thoughtful of the two. Aykroyd, however, regularly brought the argument to an abrupt but shockingly humorous halt with the now infamous words, "Jane, you ignorant slut!"

The idea of the Point-Counter Point persuasive speech is similar. In this case, however, only one person is doing the talking. The speaker presents the points of an accepted or proposed argument and then destroys said points with new and more persuasive arguments.

The important thing to remember if you want to successfully use the point-counter point design for persuasion is that not only do you need to show the weakness in you opponent's position you must also clearly demonstrate that your points and/or proposals are better.

For example, one of my students recently confronted the opponents of the war in Iraq by acknowledging their position, showing the apparent weakness of their arguments and then eradicating them with what he believed were new and stronger arguments of his own.

Motivated Sequence. Perhaps, the simplest and most effective design for persuasion is Monroe's Motivated Sequence. Alan Monroe, a former professor of Speech and Public Speaking at Purdue University developed this design in 1935 and it is still used by novices and pros alike because of its powerful ability to motivate an audience. When used well, the motivated sequence is the most efficacious of all designs for motivating audiences to take action—to do something. Perhaps what makes Monroe's Motivated Sequence so effective is that not only is it a more sophisticated problem-solution design, but it is also closely aligned with the process of persuasion that takes place within the audience (awareness, acceptance, retention, and action) and that we discussed in the previous chapter.

There are basically five steps or stages in the motivated sequence design that need to be developed fully and proportionately. That is, each should have approximately the same weight and impact on your audience.

1. Capture Attention. As in any speech, the first step is to gain the audience's attention. (At this point, you may want to review the subject of Introductions in Chapter 10)   However, your attention-getting introduction must connect with the issue you are about to raise for your audience as in the following example from a speech in which the speaker was asking the audience to become an organ donor.

How many of you have signed an organ donor card or have stated on your license that in the event of a tragedy you would be willing to donate your organs so that someone else might live? It may be a scary question for you. Something you really don't like to think about. After all, who likes to think about dying? Well, I was driving down the road the other day and saw a car with a bumper sticker that took me back to a personal event that changed my life. You've probably seen the bumper sticker too. It says: "Don't take your organs to heaven—Heaven knows we need them here!"

2. Demonstrate the Need. This second step is your opportunity to show the audience where the problem lies. Be clear and precise about the problem. Don't leave the audience wondering what you are really trying to say. You also want to make sure that you can demonstrate the extent of the problem with both verifiable knowledge (facts, statistics, expert testimony, etc.) and by showing your audience why it is pertinent to them as in this example from a speech on becoming an organ donor:

When used well, the motivated sequence is the most efficacious of all designs for motivating audiences to take action – to do something.

Maybe you've never considered the lack of organ donors in this country a problem. I know I never thought about it. Sure, I remember seeing something on ER last season. And I think when I renewed my driver's license someone asked me if I wanted to sign the back and become an organ donor. But I never really thought about it. Not until I got that telephone call a couple of years ago. The call that no one ever forgets. It was from my mother. Her voice sounded tired and shaky. Not like her normal self at all. She called me early one Tuesday morning to tell me that Dad had gone into congestive heart failure. They were waiting. Waiting for a word about a transplant and that I should come home right away. That's when it got real for me. That's when I started digging around for answers. Did you know that according to the U.S. Health and Human Services there are over 83,000 people waiting. Waiting for organs to become available. 83,000 people. That's the size of a small city. Just waiting. 83,000 people hoping they live long enough to hear the telephone ring with good news instead of bad. I imagine it's hard to stay hopeful. In October 2003 there were 19,000 transplants done in this country but only 9,800 new donors. Do the math—the numbers don't add up. And according to the National Kidney Foundation "because of the lack of available donors in the United States, 2,025 kidney patients, 1,347 liver patients, 458 heart patients and 361 lung patients died in 2001 while waiting

> To persuade is to provide the opportunity and the understanding necessary for your audience to make an informed, wise, and favorable decision.

for life-saving organ transplants." Those are grave statistics for far too many people - 4191 people every year to be exact. Especially if it is your father or mother - or brother or sister - who is the one desperately waiting by the telephone.

3. Satisfy the Need. In this third step, the speaker is going to turn the audience away from bad news and toward good. This is where you will provide a solution to the problem or an answer to the question. Again, you want to make sure that your proposal is as clear and precise as the need that you have just demonstrated. Back up your proposal with both verifiable and personal knowledge. Make sure to deal with any counter arguments you may anticipate from the audience. And show your audience that you are willing to practice what you preach!

> *Well look, it doesn't have to be this way. By signing a donor card or the back of our licenses, each and every one of us can make a difference. If we just raised the number of donors by five or ten percent, it could make the difference between death and life for thousands of people - people like my father, or like your father or even like you or me. People with real names and faces. People we know and love. Mother Theresa once said that to change the world, we don't have to do great things; just small things with great love. This could be one of the greatest acts of love we ever make. To save a human life. And don't worry that signing your card means that doctors won't treat you if you are ever seriously injured because they have another patient who needs a transplant. That's a myth. According to the U.S. Health and Human Services "Every effort is made to save your life before donation is considered." And there are very few religions that don't allow for transplants either. There's nothing stopping us from doing the right thing. I downloaded a Donor Card from Organdonor.gov and signed the day after my father's heart attack. It was that simple. A small thing done with great love!*

4. Visualize the Results. In this step, you will paint a picture of how things will look if they accept your proposal or how they will look if they don't. Please note, though, for the most part people tend to respond more to the positive than to the negative. This is not a time for scaring people into action. Remember what Eisenhower said: "If I scare him, he will stay just as long as he is scared, and then he is gone." You want your speech to have an effect even after you have finished speaking. You may want to use a personal narrative at this point or create a vivid image in the minds of your audience.

Just imagine how many telephones would be ringing with good news for donor recipients tomorrow, if every American signed a donor card or his or her license today. We may not be able to stop the number of accidents that happen, but we can stop a great deal of tragedy for those who are waiting for a call right now - even as we speak. I remember it was two weeks after my father had been placed on the National Donor Registry that our telephone rang. When we got the news that a heart had become available, my mother and my two brothers and I danced around the living room with excitement. When we came down to earth, it hit us all of a sudden: Dad would live because someone, somewhere, had died - and because they had done something completely selfless before they died: they signed their donor card. We're not a terribly religious family but right then and right there in the middle of the living room we stopped and gave thanks for the nameless person who was giving Dad a second chance on life. My father celebrated his 56th birthday last week. We talked for a long time about that amazing person whose small act, done with great love, gave my Dad his life back. Today, my father's new heart is filled with gratitude.

5. **Call to Action.** The final step is to tell your audience precisely what you want them to do. It is your last chance to connect with them in a positive way. Let them know that you have a way to make it easier for them to act by bringing copies for everyone of important websites, addresses, letters, petitions and donor cards.

It has been said: "a million deaths—a statistic; a single death— a tragedy." Don't let the huge numbers overwhelm you. When

> An eloquent
> man must speak
> so as to teach,
> to delight, and
> to persuade. To
> teach is a
> necessity, to
> delight is a
> beauty, to
> persuade is a
> triumph.
> —*Cicero*

you go to organdonor.gov and sign your donor card or sign the back of your license, it's not just a statistic that you will reduce, it's a tragedy which you will prevent. I hope the need never arises, but if it does, your last gift here on earth may be the best gift you ever give. At risk of sounding too much like a bumper sticker: Don't take your organs to heaven with you. Heaven knows we need them here. Sign your license or donor card today. Thank you.

The art and craft of persuasion is here to stay. In the words of Isocrates, because we have the power to persuade, "not only have we escaped the life of wild beasts, but we have come together and founded cities and made laws and invented arts." Great speakers have the ability to persuade ethically, and effectively.

Upon Reflection

1. Make a list of all the things people have tried to persuade you to do in the last five days. Were they successful? Why or why not?
2. Make a list of all the things you have tried to persuade others to do in the last five days. Were you successful? Why or why not?
3. Develop a short speech (1-2 minutes) with a motivated sequence design whose goal is to convince someone (in particular, if you wish) to go out on a date with you.
4. Find a friend or partner, research a hot topic and role-play Point-Counter Point.

— 14 —

The Speech of Celebration

Stop worrying about the potholes in the road
and celebrate the journey!
—Barbara Hoffman

I HAVE A FRIEND, a Roman Catholic Priest, whose greatest fear is that when he dies and goes to heaven, God will face him down with astonishment and say, "Celibate? I didn't say, 'Celibate.' I said 'Celebrate!'"

What would life be without our celebrations? Our celebrations are an important and integral part of our lives part. Oprah Winfrey once said that, "the more you praise and celebrate your life, the more there is in life to celebrate." Whether it be the celebration of a marriage following a wedding or the celebration of a life on the occasion of a loved one's death, the words we use to celebrate knit us together in community as people with a common experience.

Our celebrations usually surround rites of passage or milestones on the journey. The words we use at these times help mark the occasion. Our words name the occasion for us and help us focus on the real reason we are celebrating. We lift our glasses in a toast, not to just to drink or get drunk, but to mark and honor this moment, this event, or this person. Our words and speeches are the cornerstone of celebration; they identify meaning and assist us in commemorating an event.

Articulation

During times of celebration it is important for the speaker to help those who have gathered articulate their own inner feelings about the significance of the event. Good speeches aid in uncovering, at deeper levels, the reason or reasons for the celebration. In short, our speeches of celebration name why we are celebrating. You have probably heard the phrase "Dearly Beloved, we are gathered here today to . . ." This is a formal way of naming the story that we are all living. You will likely find more informal and imaginative ways of telling your audience why you all have come together, as in the following student speech that began a class of student celebration speeches:

> *Good afternoon and welcome to the 14th session of Dr. Mark Giuliano's Speech and Public Speaking Class. We are gathered here to share our voices in celebration, to speak and communicate, to listen and to concentrate. We have come here to offer our humble speeches of celebration, commemoration, edification, inspiration and even adoration! Today we will stand up one by one and have some fun, to speak our minds and outlined lines. But this is why we are here as a group. Every one of us has come for individual reasons too: For some, we're here because it's required. For some, we're here to be a better speaker. And still, for others, we're here today because we've already missed the maximum of four classes because we were too nervous to give our informative speech and freaked out a little. Luckily, I came back. And now I am glad you are willing to listen to me . ..*
>
> (Adapted from Dylan Johnson's tribute speech to his speech class)

Magnification

How many times in our daily lives do we focus our attention on one specific person or event? Not many. How often is attention focused specifically on us? Since the day we ceased to be 'cute-as-a-button' children, even less. The Greek rhetorician, Aristotle pointed out that to focus attention on an individual or his or her achievements in life, is to magnify them in the minds of the audience. This can happen quite naturally as we turn the attention of our audience specifically toward the one(s) being honored.

CAUTION! You don't need to exaggerate. Audiences can smell exaggeration a mile away. It makes you sound like a phony. A funeral director friend of mine once joked, "Mark, I've seen too many saints born on the day of their funeral!" Just keep it real and keep it focused on the person or event at hand and you will achieve magnification, as in the following excerpt from a tribute speech to British fashion editor for Vogue Magazine, Grace Coddington:

> *Tonight . . . I have the honor of presenting an amazing woman the award for Thirty Years of Fashion at Vogue Magazine. She was born a jewel to rise and sparkle in the glimmering world of fashion - a bright center stone in a setting of high fashion and glamour.*
>
> (Adapted from a student a speech by fashion major,
> Amanda C. Vaughn)

Unification

Speeches of celebration also unite the audience in the common experience around which they have gathered. For example, in a wedding speech, the speaker will bring together two families, two sets of friends—two stories which otherwise would remain estranged.

By using stories or recollections, you help your audience identify with you, each other and the cause for celebration. The stories or recollections we hold in common, when spoken aloud, hold a power that unite us. Speeches of celebration are the perfect opportunity to tell a moving narrative, humorous anecdote or relate a personal achievement as in the following example continued from above:

> *Before I present this award . . . I would like to venture back to the beginning. It all started when an eyebrow arched, bouffant hairdo woman glided onto the stage of fashion and dropped her fur coat, tweaking the assurance of such names as Vidal Sassoon and Calvin Klein. By 1964, she had succeeded in transforming herself*

into an independent, free thinking and bold spirited woman who won the respect and attention of many great photographers and fashion icons.

(Adapted from a speech by fashion major, A. C. Vaughn)

Inspiration

Inspiration is a key element to many celebration speeches. In times of grief and loss, such as a funeral, the eulogy (see Speeches of Tribute further in this chapter) can inspire hope and courage. Before a big game, a coach may offer words that inspire his or her team to play on to victory. At a wedding reception, a speaker may inspire the bride and groom with words of encouragement for the long road of marriage ahead. Politicians often use inspiration as a way of encouraging loyal followers and attracting new ones. Inspiration usually reminds audiences of what they have already accomplished and what they can accomplish together. The following speech was made by William Wallace (Mel Gibson) to the Scottish Army at Stirling in the 1995 movie *Braveheart*:

Wallace: Sons of Scotland, I am William Wallace.

Young soldier: William Wallace is 7 feet tall.

Wallace: Yes, I've heard. Kills men by the hundreds, and if he were here he'd consume the English with fireballs from his eyes and bolts of lightning from his arse. I am William Wallace. And I see a whole army of my countrymen here in defiance of tyranny. You have come to fight as free men, and free men you are. What would you do without freedom? Will you fight?

Veteran soldier: Fight? Against that? No, we will run; and we will live.

Wallace: Aye, fight and you may die. Run and you'll live -- at least a while. And dying in your beds many years from now, would you be willing to trade all the days from this day to that for one chance, just one chance to come back here and tell our enemies that they may take our lives, but they'll never take our freedom.

Wallace and Soldiers: Alba gu bra! (Scotland forever!)

Edification

At a much deeper level, speeches of celebration honor the sacred river of life that is always flowing just beneath the surface of our gatherings. Our speeches recognize and attempt to name that which is holy, or beautiful or true, but is always just beyond the reach of our meager words. And yet, we make our attempt to edify a deep and existential moment - to celebrate not just another event but the eternal, mysterious and sacred event that underscores our lives.

Of course, this is not an easy thing to do. So we turn to the poets and lyricists. We speak in metaphor and analogy, rhyme and meter. And even then, our words, after drawing back the curtain for a brief glimpse of life's sacred beauty, will fall just short of naming what refuses to be named. But in the end, maybe it is in our humble attempt that we are most inextricably woven together in human community.

Rev. Dr. Martin Luther King, Jr. was masterful at helping us see truth and beauty in the midst of chaos, even if he had to tell us of dreams or draw from biblical allusions atop soaring mountains:

> *We've got some difficult days ahead. But it really doesn't matter with me now, because I've been to the mountaintop... And I've looked over, and I've seen the Promised Land. I may not get there with you. But I want you to know tonight, that we, as a people, will get to the Promised Land. So I'm happy tonight; I'm not worried about anything; I'm not fearing any man. Mine eyes have seen the glory of the coming of the Lord.*
>
> (Martin Luther King Jr., Memphis, April 3, 1968,
> the day before his assassination.)

Four Types of Celebration Speeches

1. *Speeches of Introduction:*

> *"Good afternoon and welcome. My name is Cuyler Hovey-King and I would like to thank you for joining us today at the*

Trustee's Theater in beautiful Savannah, Georgia to explore the work of Sarah Perkins, who as many of you may already know, or for those who don't know, is a renowned contemporary metal-smith specializing in unconventional hollow formed vessels. She has been kind enough to accept our invitation to come to the Savannah College of Art and Design all the way from the Show Me State — Missouri — where she is currently an Associate Professor in the Department of Art and Design at Southwest Missouri State University." (Adapted from Cuyler Hovey-King's student introduction speech.)

Okay so you have been asked to introduce the guest speaker at the Rotary luncheon or the guest lecturer for your school's quarterly symposium. You need to know what to do and you need to know quickly. What do you do? Regardless of the occasion, the principles of introduction are basically the same.

Make Sure You Know How to Pronounce the Speaker's Name. I can't tell you how many times my name has been mispronounced. You'd think since people were paying all that money to get me to come and speak they might want to get the name right!

Find Out If There Is Something the Guest Speaker would like you to bring to the audience's attention. Is there some sort of special anecdote or some important information that will help things go more smoothly?

Help Focus the Audience's Attention Toward the Subject. You can do the guest speaker and the audience a great big favor by introducing the topic to the audience before hand.

Make the Guest Speaker Feel Welcome. Offer some honest and genuine comments about the speaker. Let the audience and the guest speaker know just how pleased everyone is that he or she is with you today.

Help Build Up the Speaker's Ethos. Remind the audience of what a great person, scholar, or even exceptional speaker they are going to hear from on this particular occasion. This might require you to do a little research in preparation for your guest speaker's visit.

Thank the Guest Speaker for Being There. An expression of gratitude is essential. Thoughtful and well-planned words of thanks honor your guest.

Be Brief! It is pretty embarrassing if the introduction speech goes longer than the guest speaker's speech!

2. Toasts and Roasts—Speeches of Tribute

> *Pierre Elliot Trudeau was a man like no other. A man of brilliance and learning. A man of action. A man of grace and style. A man of wit and playfulness. A man of extraordinary courage. A complex man, whose love of Canada was pure and simple. Pierre wrote about "a man who never learned patriotism in school, but who acquired that virtue when he felt in his bones the vastness of his land and the greatness of its founders." Pierre, too, came to love this land as he climbed its mountain peaks, conquered the rapids of its rivers and wandered the streets of its cities . . . Pierre Trudeau was a giant of our times. And a great Canadian . . . . Pierre, you made us young. You made us proud. You made us dream. Thank you, dear friend. And farewell.*
>
> (Excerpts from a eulogy to former Canadian Prime Minister, The Right Honorable Pierre Elliot Trudeau by The Right Honorable, Jacques Jean Chrétien September 29, 2000)

Tribute speeches are our way of honoring someone on special occasions such as an award presentation (professional, artistic, sports, etc.), the occasion of a retirement, a wedding, birthday or anniversary, or at the death of a loved one in a celebration of life. At a wedding, the tribute is most often a toast. When someone has died, it is called a eulogy. When you honor someone with playful teasing, humorous exaggeration or blatant lies, it is called a roast. Here are some things to keep in mind when you deliver a tribute speech.

Focus on the Person Being Honored and Not Yourself. Remember, this speech is not about you. Far too often speakers say too much about themselves and not enough about the person being esteemed. It usually happens when the speaker is nervous, trying to be funny, has had too much to drink or a combination of the three!

As a pastor, I have sat through more agonizing, self-aggrandizing speeches by intoxicated groomsmen than I care to remember. One speech in particular was a rambling fifteen-minute exposé of the groom's pre-marital affairs offered by his drunken best man. It was supposed to be a toast to the bride and the groom. The groom tried to smile politely as his best man bumbled through story after embarrassing story about their many exploits together. The bride, upon hearing stories more suited to a stag party roast, wanted to crawl under the table. Everyone else just wanted to leave.

Don't end up sounding like Steve Buscemi's ridiculous character in the movie, *The Wedding Singer*. It's not about you! So stay sober and stay focused on the person or people you have come to honor with your words.

Share Some Personal Stories. While the stories need not always involve you, they should be personal.

Use Your Imagination. You are honoring someone with your words. Why not use your words to their full potential with some well-crafted literary devices or by using a thoughtful or interesting quote. We honor people with our choice of words, our well-crafted speeches, and our heartfelt deliveries. If we were painters honoring someone with our paintings, we would not dare whip up something at the last minute. We would spend whatever time it took to get it right prior to giving the gift. As speakers, our words are our art. We must use them skillfully and lovingly.

No Need to Exaggerate. As previously mentioned, you don't need to lie, exaggerate or otherwise blow things out of proportion. You don't want to sound like you never knew the person you are talking about.

3. Speeches of Acceptance

Every now and then, we are fortunate enough to get to deliver an acceptance speech for an award, recognition, or victory. Maybe one day you will receive a Grammy or an Oscar, Teacher of the Year or Volunteer of the Month. You may think it may never happen to you, but on the off chance that it does, be prepared!

Be Modest. One of the best introductions to an acceptance speech I have heard was from a man who began his speech humbly by saying:

> *I really don't deserve this honor. But there have been many times in my life I have taken blame for things I didn't deserve either. So tonight my philosophy is this: even if you don't deserve the honor—go ahead and accept it!*

Say "Thank You!" You didn't get this far all on your own. If you think that you did, examine your belly button and think again. All along the way there are people who have helped us get to the place we are today. Hint: if you are going to thank people by name, make sure you get them all. Otherwise, you may want to offer a blanket thanks, with special thanks to one or two very important people.

Tell Them Why You Are Thankful. You may want to tell your audience what it means to you to win the award or receive the recognition. Julie Gold, the woman who wrote the song *From a Distance*, did this extremely well in her 1991 Grammy Award acceptance speech for Song Writer of the Year. She talked about her self-doubts as a songwriter throughout the many lean years of songwriting. At times, she didn't even think of herself as a songwriter. She had a hard time believing in herself. And then one day, she got a telephone call telling her that Bette Midler was interested in covering one of her songs. By winning the Grammy, she felt that she could now truly call herself a songwriter.

4. Inspiration: Dream the Impossible Dream

Whether it is a young couple needing encouragement as they begin their married life together or a community of friends grieving the loss of a loved one, sooner or later we all need and appreciate inspirational words of comfort and hope. Sometimes we need to be challenged and told that not only should we aspire to greater things but, indeed, we are capable of it.

The word "inspire" comes from a Latin word *spiritus*, which was originally the word both for "spirit" and "breath." To inspire an audience means to breathe life or a spirit into them. To do this you need to:

Use Metaphor. Use metaphor and other strong images that speak to the deeper self. David Buttrick of Vanderbilt University once wrote, "If we genuinely wish to open up our interior life to ourselves or to others, we will turn to making metaphor." How else could we talk of abstract concepts such as hope or courage or love?

Tell the Tales of Heroes. Sometimes the best way to inspire an audience is to tell the stories of ordinary men and women who have risen above the challenges and done extraordinary things.

Speak with Passion. As with persuasive speaking, audiences respond favorably to speakers whose delivery exhibit passion and conviction. If it sounds like you believe it, chances are, your audience will too.

And Now for Something Completely Different

Graham Chapman, co-author of the 'Parrot Sketch,' is no more. He has ceased to be, bereft of life, he rests in peace, he has kicked the bucket, hopped the twig, bit the dust, snuffed it, breathed his last, and gone to meet the Great Head of Light Entertainment in the sky, and I guess that we're all thinking how sad it is that a man of such talent, such capability and kindness, of such intelligence should now be so suddenly spirited away at the age of only forty-eight, before he'd achieved many of the things of which he was capable, and before he'd had enough fun.

Well, I feel that I should say, "Nonsense. Good riddance to him, the freeloading bastard! I hope he fries." And the reason I think I should say this is, he would never forgive me if I didn't, if I threw away this opportunity to shock you all on his behalf. Anything for him but mindless good taste. . . . It is mag-nificent, isn't it? You see, the thing about shock . . . is not that it upsets some people, I think; I think that it gives others a momentary joy of liberation, as we realized in that instant that the social rules that constrict our lives so terribly are not actually very important.

Well, Gray can't do that for us anymore. He's gone. He is an ex-Chapman. All we have of him now is our memories. But it will be some time before they fade." (An Excerpt from John Cleese's Memorial Tribute to Graham (Gray) Chapman, from Monty Python Pages Dot Com (www.montypython-pages.com ©2001-2004, Damian Steele)

Upon Reflection

1. Visit American Rhetoric and read some great speeches from some great movies or submit one of your own favorites: http://www.americanrhetoric.com/moviespeeches.htm.

2. Visit Monty Python Pages at www.montypythonpages.com and read John Cleese's entire eulogy to Graham Chapman. Caution, the language may offend some people.

3. Prepare a toast to your favorite musician or actor.

4. Prepare and acceptance speech for an award you would love to win.

5. Write your own eulogy.

Part Four

The Audience

— 15 —

Connecting with Your Audience

IT HAS BEEN SAID that since we have two ears and only one mouth we should listen twice as much as we speak. Connecting with an audience depends greatly on our ability to listen to people and understand their needs. Knowing an audience is the heart of motivation and persuasion. Plato put it this way: "Orators have to learn the difference of human souls."

In this chapter we will look at three ways of understanding and relating to an audience: Maslow's Hierarchy of Needs, Demographics and the Aristotelian Proofs for persuasion.

> The Wizard: *Silence! The Great and Powerful Oz knows why you have come. Step forward. . . You dare to come to me for a heart, do you? You clinking, clanking, clattering collection of caliginous...junk! And you, Scarecrow, have the effrontery to ask for a brain? You billowing bale of bovine fodder! . . . The beneficent Oz has every intention of granting your requests! But first, you must prove yourselves worthy by performing a very small task. Bring me the broomstick of the Witch of the West.*
>
> Tin Man: *B-B-B-B-B-But if we do that, we'll have to kill her to get it!*
>
> The Wizard: *Bring me her broomstick, and I'll grant your requests. Now, go!*
>
> From the film, *The Wizard of Oz.*

Motivated By Needs and Wants

Why were Dorothy, Scarecrow, Tin Man and the Cowardly Lion all willing to risk their lives, even commit manslaughter, to pro-

Self-Actualization

Esteem and Competence

Love and Belonging

Safety and Security

Physiological

Each of the characters from *The Wizard of Oz* had a need. Interestingly, their needs corresponded to *Maslow's Hierarchy of Needs:* Dorothy needed a home (Safety and Security), Tin Man longed for a heart (Love and Belonging), the cowardly Lion desired courage (Esteem) and Scare Crow sought a brain (Competence).

Think of Maslow's Hierarchy of Needs like a ladder. We can climb higher as more fundamental needs are first met.

cure the broomstick of the Wicked Witch of the West? Was it because they had a strong sense of justice and the witch was just plain bad and needed to be dealt with? Or were they just in the mood for a little adventure? It certainly wasn't because they were in need of a broomstick for themselves.

No. Dorothy and her three unusual friends were willing to risk life and limb in the witch's castle because they each had a need which they desired to have fulfilled: a brain; a heart, the courage, a home. People are generally motivated by the possibility of having their needs met.

Abraham Maslow, the Twentieth Century American psychologist, developed a theory of motivation called a hierarchy of needs. Maslow argued that people are motivated by their needs and that fundamental needs must be met before the proposal of secondary needs can be offered. The desire to meet higher needs rests upon the fulfillment of more essential needs. When our fundamental needs are met, we can then reach for higher goals. Think of the Maslow's hierarchy of needs like a ladder; we have to climb the lower rungs before we can grab hold of the higher ones and eventually reach the top.

For example, it would be difficult to persuade a person to take up an altruistic pursuit, if his or her basic needs such as water or shelter are not first met, or to interest someone in love if his or her need for food has not been satisfied. Maybe that's why we have the old saying, "the way to a man's heart is through his stomach." Make sure the basic needs are fulfilled and then you can motivate people toward some of the unmet higher needs.

Maslow's hierarchy reflects needs in the following ascending order of importance: physiological, safety and security, love and belonging, competence and esteem, self-actualization and curiosity. Each need rests on the securing of a previous one.

Physiological Needs. Everyone needs the basics: potable water to drink, clean air to breathe, good food to eat, a roof over our heads and clothing to protect us from the elements. We need intimacy, health, and ease of suffering. When any of these are missing, we are motivated to resolve them. For example, I once had a student who apologized for missing class because he was out looking for an apartment. In other words, his motivation to meet his need for competence (level 4) was diminished greatly by his basic physiological need for shelter.

Safety and Security Needs. Once our physiological needs are satisfied, we tend to be motivated by the need for safety and security. All human beings desire both emotional and physical safety. We need safety and security through home and family life and have developed a sophisticated set of laws to protect us in our communities and in our civil lives. People who live in fear are not much interested in anything else except protection or survival. Many marketers play on our fears. Just prior to Y2K, a myriad of survival gear was sold to Americans. And just after 9-11, gun sales increased throughout America. In my own neighborhood, after a series of crimes had been reported in the local newspaper and on the nightly news, an aggressive alarm company sent young salespeople door to door to cash in on people's need for safety and security.

Love and Belonging. However, if our need for safety is met, then we are open to the possibility of love. We can respond to that deep human need to be needed and the need to belong. If our basic needs are being met and we are not afraid to go out of the house, we are free to get involved in our surrounding community through church, clubs and organizations.

Humans are relational beings. We like to belong. Television commercials not only use sex to motivate us, they also show images of people enjoying good times together. Love and belonging are quite motivational among college students who are often living away from home for the first time and working hard at fitting in. But in a world where people are moving further away from home and family and moving more often than ever before, belonging is important to many people. "An Army of One" and "The Few, The Proud, The Marines," are both slogans intended to appeal to our need to belong. It is interesting to note that just a few years prior, the U.S. Army tried to appeal to higher needs: "We Don't Ask for Experience, We Give It" appealed to our need for competence and esteem, while the slogans, "It's Not Just a Job, It's an Adventure" and "Be all That You Can Be" appealed to our need for self-actualization.

Competence and Esteem. Not only do we need to be needed, but we also like to be acknowledged and affirmed. For some, this can be simple recognition from immediate family and friends. For others, recognition from peers and colleagues is very important. And still for others, fame is a driving factor. In the end, however, all of us need the sense of accomplishment that affirms who we are and what we do.

Self-Actualization and Altruism. Be all that you can be! If all our basic needs are being met, we are usually motivated by a desire for spiritual or altruistic pursuits. Only when we are sure that other needs are being met, however, are we free enough to work for self-actualization. If we are desperate to find a job, or are working unusually long hours in fear that we won't have enough money to get by, we likely won't respond well to pleas for us to commit to on-going volunteerism. However, if our fundamental needs have been met and we feel a sense of belonging and competence in the world, we will likely want to aspire to greater things.

Demographics

Another way to connect with your audience is to consider the demographic composition of our audience members. That is to say, the part of the population they represent. There are a number of demographic considerations that might help you decide the best way to motivate your audience.

Age. How would you deliver a speech on nutrition to a group of senior citizens? I bet it would be different from the way you would talk to a group of teenagers. I like music and make a lot of musical references when I speak. If I was speaking to an audience that was made up of a lot of "baby boomers" (people born between, roughly, 1946—1960), I might quote the Beatles, Simon and Garfunkel or Bob Dylan. Whereas, if the audience had more "Gen-X"ers (people born between 1961—1980), I would probably make references to U2, Sarah McLaughlin or the Barenaked Ladies.

People of different ages may share some things in common but also have different heroes, entertainers, films, music, experiences and, especially, histories. For example, for one generation of Americans, December 7th, the anniversary of the bombing of Pearl Harbor, is a day that will never be forgotten. For others, November 22 the day President John F. Kennedy was shot, is significant. For others, it is April 4th, the day Martin Luther King was assasinated. The more you know about the age of your audience, the more intentional you will be about selecting your topic and supporting materials.

Gender. Are men and women different? Definitely. Are they different in every way? Of course not. Knowing what makes men and women different is important to motivation. The challenge speakers face in this rapidly changing world when it comes to gender, however, is knowing how to discern important differences.

How do we do this? First, after you have spent some time with the opposite sex simply listening and observing, it is important to be able access statistical data as it pertains to your topic and the gender in question. Is it important and is it reliable information? You might also read a book or two that might help you bridge the gap between women who are, allegedly, from Venus and men who are, allegedly, from Mars.

Make sure, though, not to get caught up in stereotypes. Not only is stereotyping ineffective, it can also turn an audience hostile! I once had a student who gave a speech on the subject of "10-Second Cars," (cars, usually imports, that can travel a quarter of a mile in under ten seconds) who isolated half his audience by beginning his speech with these anger-inciting words,

Now I don't mean to bore the women in the audience today, but I am going to talk to you about a subject that you are probably not very interested in: cars.

When the student finished his speech, I thought the women in the class were going to lynch him! According to a quick survey we conducted in class, not only did these college-age women have as many cars as the men and had purchased more new cars than men, but also there was even one female student who drove an aspiring 10-second car! According to Bureau of Transportation Statistics, in the year 2001, there were almost an equal number of licensed female drivers and male drivers on the road (90,951,708 males and 90,928,758 females). Don't let a lack of gender information get you in trouble!

Ethnicity. A person's ethnic background may be of greater or lesser importance to other demographic considerations depending on the subject at hand. It is important to develop an understanding of an audience's ethnic background. Are there statistical differences that are relevant to your topic? Are there significant cultural markers (books, films, music, etc.) pertaining to your audience's specific or dominant ethnicity that will help you inform or and persuade. As with age, this group may be motivated by different heroes, cultural experiences and histories. For example, some audiences may care less about what Abraham Lincoln once said or even know who he was. For some ethnic groups, family traditions will be different from your own and, perhaps, more important to them than yours are to you. Before you write your speech, seize the opportunity to learn about your audience's ethnic make-up and background.

Economic Status. How much money people make or don't make will not necessarily affect the way they think. However, it may limit what they can or cannot do. For example, it may not make much sense to try to persuade people who are just barely making ends meet to invest in a time-share or take a European vacation this summer.

Other Considerations. Other demographic considerations may include an audience's educational level, religious affiliation or political orientation. Make sure you are taking the time needed to discover who your audience is before you start writing your speech.

The Aristotelian Proofs

Twenty three hundred years ago, a Greek philosopher by the name of Aristotle (see Chapter 4) noted that audiences respond to three particular forms of rhetoric called proofs: ethos, logos and pathos. The most effective speakers use all three.

Ethos. Previously we talked about the importance of a speaker's ethos in securing audience attention. This would be a good time to review! After all, when it comes to relating to an audience, ethos is critical. Do you seem like someone who is willing to practice what you preach? Do you seem like someone who can be trusted? Do you seem competent? Are you ethical, honest and dependable? If you want to teach or persuade, you should be able to answer "yes" to these questions. Isocrates put it this way: The argument which is made by a man's life is of more weight than that which is furnished by his words. What kind of argument do you make with your personal character?

Logos. If you want to sound like a pro then sound like you know! If you want to teach or persuade an audience you will need to win the audience's approval with sound reasoning and verifiable knowledge. The word "logic" comes from logos. Your ideas will need to be logical and supported with demonstrable evidence as in the following example on "Saying No" to the use of the synthetic drug called Ecstasy:

Now I'm not just talking about my opinion here. The facts tell an equally serious story: According to the National Institute on Drug Abuse (NIDA), people who use Ecstasy "may encounter problems similar to those experienced by amphetamine and cocaine users, including addiction." NIDA states that Ecstasy use can lead to "confusion, depression, sleep problems, anxiety, and paranoia during, and sometimes weeks after, taking the drug." And the physical effects are just as alarming. Ecstasy users may experience "muscle tension, involuntary teeth-clenching, nausea, blurred vision, faintness, and chills or sweating." It increases both heart rate and blood pressure that, after prolonged use, can lead to heart failure and other heart diseases. Ecstasy destroys brain serotonin neurons necessary for regulating our mood, memory, sleep, and appetite. Moreover, recent research shows that ecstasy use causes permanent memory loss.

Teching and persuading people takes more than opinion; it takes solid evidence.

Pathos. Pathos is that gentle tug on the heartstring that creates an emotional connection between your audience and your subject. The word itself, pathos, means "feeling." It is where we get English words like "sympathy." Aristotle rightly argued that if we are going to connect with our audiences we will need to elicit from them or inspire within them, some degree of sympathy, compassion or empathy. You can do this by using powerful images, telling a moving story or relaying a personal experience as in the following example continued from above:

> *The problem of ecstasy hit home for me and my family one evening last spring or should I say early morning. That's when the police showed up at our door to tell my parents that my little sister, Morgan, had been rushed to the hospital after experiencing a kind of seizure at a high school party—a rave. Her boyfriend had got her to try ecstasy for the first time. He said it wouldn't hurt her to try it just once, but it did. Morgan says all that she can remember is feeling something like a panic attack: her heart beating fast and hard, her body breaking out in a clammy sweat. The room seemed fuzzy. Then she lost consciousness all together . . .*

In this example, a proper name, Morgan, is used to make the story even more personal. To inform or motivate an audience you need to call on the audience's sense of compassion.

Mythos. Although Aristotle did not include mythos as one of the important proofs for communication, orators in modern times have identified it as a powerful tool in relating to an audience. Mythos is the use of myth or folk tale as a way of answering deep or ultimate questions, as in the Chinese story of the stonecutter:

> *All day Lei labored under the hot sun, hammering away at the mountain to bring rock and gravel to his community. Lei saw what power the sun had and so he prayed to the gods and said, "I pray that I was the sun then I would have its power and*

would not have to toil under its heat all day." The gods granted him his prayer and Lei became the sun. And he was happy for a while. But soon a cloud came and covered up the sun and blocked out its powerful heat. So Lei asked the gods to let him be a cloud so that he could have more power than the sun. Again, the gods granted him his prayer and Lei became a cloud. And he was happy for a while. But soon the wind came and blew the cloud over the mountain that made the cloud begin to rain. Lei saw what power the mountain had and so Lei asked the gods to let him become the mountain so that he would have more power than the sun or the clouds. Again, the gods granted him his prayer and Lei became the mountain. And he was happy for a while. Until he felt the blows of a stone cutter hammering away at the base of the mountain, eating him away bit by bit. Lei prayed to the gods to let him be a stonecutter once again, but the gods did not answer him. (Source unknown)

If you want to connect with people, know who they are. Know what their needs are. In the words of Plato, "learn the difference in human souls."

Upon Reflection

1. In one column, make a list of your needs. In another, make a list of your wants. What is your greatest need right now?
2. What kind of cultural images, heroes, entertainers, films, music, experiences or stories would you use to persuade a group of high school students to get more physically active?
3. What kind of cultural images, heroes, entertainers, films, music, experiences or stories would you use to persuade a group of senior citizens to get more physically active?
4. Find someone of a different gender or ethnicity and interview him or her about their childhood. What do you have in common? What was different?

5. What sort of folk tales or myths can you recall? Do they have a message?
6. Visit www.ocbtracker.com/ladypixel/legend and read the legends of the Blackfeet and the Kiowa.

— 16 —

Etiquette and Ethics

*Stand up for what is right, even if you
feel like you're standing alone.*

YOU MIGHT SAY SPEECH etiquette is just the ticket for speaking in public. After all, quite literally, that's what etiquette means. The word "etiquette" is French for "ticket." Many years ago the term was ascribed to a small card with written instructions telling people how to behave in court. Eventually it came to mean what it does today, a non-binding code of conduct for social or professional situations. There are different rules of etiquette in every culture. Being aware of those rules will be most helpful if we are speaking out of our own context.

Ethics, on the other hand, comes from the same Greek root as, you guessed it, ethos which, as we know now, pertains to ones personal character or morals. In the plural, ethics mean the science or principles of morality. In the western world, at risk of over simplifying a complex subject, our ethics and the laws that govern them, have come to us by way of Judeo/Christian laws (such as the Ten Commandments, other Mosaic laws, the golden rule and other teachings of Jesus) and Greco/Roman philosophies (such as Aristotle's Ethics). And, as you can imagine, in our highly pluralistic culture, our system of ethics continues to evolve.

When it comes to public speaking, etiquette and ethics are akin to one another. However, etiquette is something speakers do out of politeness and respect for the audience; whereas, ethics pertains to those things which are expected.

The Five Principles of Speech Etiquette

1. Honor thy audience. The audience is the most important concern for public speakers. Not only will it help you get the attention off yourself, if you are an anxious speaker, it will send out a very clear signal to your audience that you are someone likeable and trustworthy.

2. *Honor thyself.* One of the ways we honor an audience is by honoring ourselves. Dress appropriately for the occasion and the subject of your speech. Even in a classroom situation, you should be dressed at least little bit better than your audience.

3. *Honor the gift of thy language.* Use language appropriate to the situation. The more formal the occasion, or the more serious the subject, the more formal your language should be. As I reminded you in Chapter 14, we honor our audience with our skillful use of language. Tell your audience that you respect them enough to have crafted an interesting speech in both form and content. This means you want to make it as interesting as possible by using effective literary devices, images, narratives, thoughtful quotes and helpful facts and statistics within the form of an intentional and well-planned speech design.

4. *Honor thy time.* People will be giving you a certain amount of their time. Make sure to use it wisely by composing and delivering a well-written speech. Don't waste the audience's time by just "winging it." If you have been given five minutes to speak, then finish within five minutes. If you think you have more than five minutes worth of information to talk about then think again! Go back and pare down your speech. If you are going to honor an audience and the event where you are speaking, then you will have to honor the prescribed time. It is not fair to other speakers or items on the agenda if you take more than what is offered.

5. *Honor thy words.* In spite of the big lie we were all taught as children: sticks and stones may break my bones, but names will never hurt me, the truth of the matter is that our words have a powerful, devastating and lasting effect. We need to choose them and use them carefully and wisely.

The Ten Commandments of Speech Ethics

1. *Thou Shalt Not Stereotype.* Put simply, stereotyping is judging an entire group of people based on the impressions formed by the words or actions of individuals within that group. For example, just because some men don't like to stop and ask for directions, doesn't mean that all men refuse to stop and ask for directions. In the last chapter, when discussing demographics, I used the example of the student who angered the women in the audience by stating that a speech on the subject of sports cars would not be interesting to women because women aren't interested in cars, period. Not only was the student wrong, he had offended half his audience!

But stereotyping has deeper consequences than offending your audience. When we stereotype, we both affirm and promote misconceptions about groups of people. Our words form meaning. And the more we hear something said, the more we are apt to believe it. As a speaker, you have the power to overturn those misconceptions by not stereotyping.

2. *Thou Shalt Not Quote Out of Context.* Speakers usually quote out of context for one of two reasons: either they are malicious and intentionally trying to deceive an audience or, more commonly, they are lazy and haven't fully researched an idea. If you are trying to mislead an audience, knock it off—you're lying. You know it and soon everyone else will too. If you are quoting out of context as a result of not having read a complete text or not having fully researched a topic, then get busy.

Too often what happens is a speaker writes a speech and then goes searching for just the right fact or quote to support his or her position. This is called proof-texting. Flipping through the pages of an article or quickly surfing the net, we find a sentence that sounds like it will support our argument. But not having done thorough research we give incomplete information to our audience. Not to mention, if our audience happens to have read more on the subject than we have, we sound like idiots!

3. *Thou Shalt Not Plagiarize.* Plagiarism is taking the work of another and claiming it as your own. It is not only unethical,

it is against the policy of every accredited educational institution in America and it is illegal. Plagiarism is a form of stealing and speakers and authors have been sued for claiming the works of another as their own, or even failing to give them proper citation.

4. Thou Shalt Not Use Sexist or Racist Remarks or Humor. Most sexist and racist humor is based on stereotypes (see above) or plain bigotry. This kind of language is unethical. Remember, our words form meaning. And when we use our words in this way we both affirm and promote misconceptions within our audience.

I remember being at a conference not too long ago. There was a speaker who was talking about effective communication for non-profit organizations. In an attempt to be witty, he concluded his speech by saying, "In the words of Dolly Parton, 'If you've got it—stick it out there.'" Not only did I doubt that Dolly Parton had actually said this, I couldn't help but notice that most women in the room were seething with anger and most men were crawling under their seats in embarrassment that one of their own had said something so sexist. You may think it is funny but it's not!

5. Thou Shalt Not Use Inflammatory Remarks. Put-downs may stir up a crowd, but they are a poor substitute for the mature, critical thinking which needs to go into a powerful and ethical speech. During an election year we learn more dirt about politicians than we care to know; and yet, we remain in the dark about the real issues. Why? Because campaign speeches and commercial sound bites are too often just cheap shots and other inflammatory remarks designed to discredit an opponent even if it means lying or using irrelevant information. The question is, do we have real issues to tackle or are we just whining?

6. Thou Shalt Not Attack Individuals. We exemplify a far greater integrity when we attack problems instead of people. For example, instead of slinging mud at the President for a record national deficit, why not consider the whole administration, its policies or even the economic trends? Speeches are not our opportunity to start name-calling. There will be times when we need to name names, however. But naming names should always happen within the context of the real issues and not just cheap shots.

7. *Thou Shalt Not Sell Out.* At the end of the day, you have to be able sleep at night. If you find yourself selling out just to keep the audience happy, you will end up hating yourself. Compromise is important in any situation, whether it be in a personal relationship or in a persuasive speech. But before you begin, decide where the line is. How much are you willing to bend before you snap?

8. *Thou Shalt Not Have Hidden Agendas.* You don't have to lay all your cards on the table at the very beginning of your speech, but you do need to clarify for the audience just what it is you are trying to persuade them to do and why. When you withhold information about your agenda, your audience grows quickly suspicious of you.

9. *Thou Shalt Not Use False or Misleading Information.* All information in your speech should be in some way verifiable. Otherwise, it is simply hearsay, opinion or outright false. Speakers who use false information are either lazy, which works against ethos, or manipulative, which cannot withstand scrutiny anyway. Be honest about your agenda. Give people the opportunity to make informed and wise decisions and you will have their attention long after the speech is over.

10. *Thou Shalt Not Pass Off Opinions as Facts.* Your opinion is important. So are facts and other verifiable information. But never confuse the two. Your opinion is what you think or believe about something but cannot prove without verifiable information. Without the supporting evidence you are just whistling "Dixie!"

Speech etiquette and speech ethics are not only expected, but in the end, if you are practicing the rules and guidelines, it will make you a more competent, trustworthy and respected speaker. Not only will audiences see you as someone with integrity, you will believe in yourself! In the words of the Chinese master, Lao Tse, "From caring comes courage."

Upon Reflection

1. Watch an infomercial on television from beginning to end and ask yourself the following questions:

   • Was I told up front what was being sold and how much it was going to cost?
   • Was I given information or was information withheld which made me suspicious of the speaker and/or the product?
   • Did I feel like I had enough information to make an informed, wise and favorable decision?
   • What would help me better make a decision?

2. Get some friends together, make popcorn, view Steve Martin's character, Jonas Nightengale in the movie, *Leap of Faith* and discuss the following questions:

   • Is Jonas Nightengale an ethical speaker?
   • Who did he fool?
   • Would he fool you? Why or why not?

3. Write an ethical 30-second commercial using Monroe's Motivated Sequence (from Chapter 13) to sell a product of your choosing.

4. Write an unethical 30-second commercial using Monroe's Motivated Sequence (from Chapter 13) to sell a product of your choosing.

5. Present numbers three and four to your friends or classmates and discuss the components that made your commercials either ethical or unethical.

— 17 —

Humor

A sense of humor is part of the art of leadership,
of getting along with people, of getting things done.
— Dwight D. Eisenhower

Where humor is concerned there are no standards.
no one can say what is good or bad,
although you can be sure that everyone will.
—John Kenneth Galbraith

ADMITTEDLY, TALKING ABOUT HUMOR is a dangerous activity. E.B. White claimed that "Analyzing humor is like dissecting a frog. Few people are interested and the frog dies of it!" And comedian-actor, Robert Benchly once said that "Defining and analyzing humor is a pastime of humorless people." But then again, weren't these humorists doing just that—talking about humor?

So I say let's throw caution to the wind and talk about it. Will we be boring, dull, or even humorless people? Probably! But on the off chance that we can pick up a few pointers and learn some things about humor which will help our speeches become more effective and entertaining, then let's go for it! After all, if you want your audience laughing with you and not at you, you will learn and practice some of the dos and don'ts of humor and public speaking.

Why Use Humor?

Why should we use humor in our speeches, anyway. Aren't our deep thoughts and moving stories enough to teach, entertain or persuade an audience? Perhaps, but if done correctly, humor can augment your efforts tenfold! Here's how:

Relax Your Audience. If you have a tough speech to give on a tough subject or if you are addressing a potentially hostile audience, humor has an intoxicating power to soothe the savage beast within your listeners! Mark Twain put it this way, "Humor is the great thing, the saving thing. The minute it crops up, all our irritations and resentments slip away and a sunny spirit takes their place." What a gift to be able to take people's gloomy skepticism and replace it with a "sunny spirit."

Relax Yourself. Not only can humor soothe the beasts in the audience, if done well, it can calm the anxiety demons within ourselves.

Build Ethos. We like to laugh. And we like people who can make us laugh. If a speaker can get us smiling or laughing periodically throughout the speech, we will likely be more attentive to what is being said and more responsive to what is being proposed.

Talk About Sticky Subjects. The saying, "behind every bit of humor there is always some truth" is an important one. Humor allows us to get at some uncomfortable or controversial truths in a subtle, indirect or less damaging way. Mary Hirsch, the Minnesotan writer, called humor "a rubber sword - it allows you to make a point without drawing blood." Sometimes, humor buffers the impact of more forceful comments that are to follow, as with Senator Zell Miller's (D—Georgia) controversial speech on current trends and morality delivered to the United States Senate on February 12, 2004:

> *"How many of you have ever run over a skunk with your car? I have many times and I can tell you, the stink stays around for a long time. You can take the car through a car wash and it's still there. So the scent of this event [Janet Jackson exposing her breast at the 2004 Super Bowl] will long linger in the nostrils of America."*

When Not to Use Humor

Are You Funny? Are You Sure? Knowing your strengths and weak-

> Humor is a rubber sword. It allows you to make a point without drawing blood.
> —*Mary Hirsch*

nesses as a speaker is important. If you know you are not funny, don't try it! Don't turn off audiences with humor that doesn't work or because your timing isn't very good. When you try to be funny but are not, you run the risk of making audiences feel embarrassed for you.

Can You Laugh at Yourself? An ability to laugh at oneself is a sign of maturity and competence. If you can laugh at yourself you send out a positive signal that you are comfortable both with the subject of your speech and with yourself. If you can't laugh at yourself, you send out a negative signal that you are inexperienced and unsure of yourself. If you can't laugh at yourself, don't make fun of anyone or anything else. It's just plain poor form.

Is This an Appropriate Context? There are times when humor is not only important, it is necessary, such as a roast. There are other contexts, however, where you will need to use some thoughtfulness to decide whether humor is appropriate or not.

Sometimes humor can go too far. I remember being at a funeral a few years back when the minister asked if anyone in the congregation would like to come to the front of the sanctuary to offer some personal words of remembrance. One or two people came forward and offered reflections that were both serious and light hearted. But as more and more people came forward, the comments seemed less and less serious and more and more contrived in an attempt to get some laughs. By the end of the service, a number of the immediate family members were visibly offended.

Are You Just Warming Up the Audience? Warming up the audience with a few jokes or humorous anecdotes used to be a standard public speaking technique. But these days, audiences can see right through the trick. They are ready for it. And unless your humor has some sort of direct correlation to your subject, it seems contrived and makes you look like a phony. Audiences are wising up and waiting for the iron fist wrapped in the velvet glove. If it doesn't connect to your subject, leave it out!

> So long as you are laughing with your audience and not at them, people are able to enjoy a broad range of humor. But remember the general rule: When in doubt, cut it out!

Humor Check List

When trying to decide whether to use a particular piece of humor,

I usually run it through a quick checklist to see if it meets the acceptable criteria. My list is as follows:

Will it Offend? Is this anecdote or other piece of humor stereotyping or will it offend someone in my audience in another way. Red flags of concern might include the various ages within an audience or the ethnic backgrounds represented. Religious or political affiliations have historically been taboo subjects for public speakers. However, with an ounce of sensitivity, you may discover that these days people are more able to laugh at their own religion and, in some circumstances, even their political persuasion so long as you are laughing with them and not at them. The general rule, however, is: when in doubt, cut it out!

Is it New or Fresh? People are more likely to enjoy the humor if they haven't already heard it a dozen times over the last two years on The Tonight Show, David Letterman and endless internet forwards! Even though we may begin a joke with the words, "Did you hear the one about . . . ?" We're hoping they haven't.

Does it Have a Ring of Truth to It? Dick Clark once humorously made the point that, "Humor is always based on a modicum of truth. Have you ever heard a joke about a father-in-law?" If it sounds disconnected from our common experience or contrived in any other way, not only will people not respond well, they will doubt our authenticity. In the audience, people will be thinking, "Uh, oh! Here comes the iron fist wrapped in the velvet glove again!"

Does it Connect to your subject? As with having a ring of truth to it, our humor should also have some sort of easily understood connection to the topic of our speech. Otherwise, you are asking people to make an artificial leap from your jokes to your subject. And in a speech, artificial means just that: artificial.

Is It in Good Taste? Your goal is to connect with the audience, not scare it away. Knowing both your audience and the context for which you will be speaking will help you determine whether your humor is going to be in good taste or not. In the last chapter I told you about a man speaking about communication in business who had ended his speech by supposedly quoting Dolly Parton,

"If you've got it, just stick it out there." He lost most of the audience and downgraded his own credibility because his humor, for that audience and that context, was in poor taste.

Is It Performable? Sometimes we may have a great story to tell but for one reason or another it just won't work with our speech. Perhaps it is too long, or it requires a volunteer when you are not quite sure you will get one. Other times we may need to adjust the story or joke so that it can be delivered easily. This is most often the case with riddles. With riddles you can't always count on someone in a large audience having courage enough to take a stab at an answer, or at least the answer for which you were hoping. So you need to reconstruct the riddle and tell it as a joke as in the following light bulb riddle told as a joke:

You don't have to live in Savannah very long to know that it takes 101 locals to change a light bulb: 50 names on a petition to the Historical Society requesting that the light be changed, one to screw in the new bulb, and another 50 to open a museum to honor the old one.

Will Everyone Get It? When I was a kid my two older brothers told great jokes that kept our neighborhood friends in hysterics. And even though I never understood half of those jokes, I would laugh along anyway. I didn't want to get caught not understanding and consequently be left out. You don't want to use humor that will leave others behind or leave them out entirely.

Is it Brief? Even if you have a longer time to deliver your speech, you don't want to drag people through a shaggy dog story. Long and winding anecdotes tend to tire out audiences. The best humor is sharp and succinct.

Humor can do many great things for your speech. It can also destroy it! Practice the principles presented here and you can't go wrong . . . probably!

Upon Reflection

1. Consider the following individual but unusual wedding day scenarios:

   - The bride is pregnant. The groom and the rest of the family, although overjoyed, just found out on the day of the wedding.
   - The groom locked keys in car and was late for his own wedding.
   - The groom passed-out from nervous exhaustion during the vows. After a brief pause the wedding continued few minutes later.
   - The bride was so nervous during the wedding vows that she forgot the groom's name.

2. How could you write a one-minute wedding toast given the above circumstances?
3. How could you use humorous vocabulary, literary devices and anecdotes to playfully make light of these circumstances?
4. How much humor, if any, would you use before it became offensive to those concerned?
5. What is your favorite joke? Why?
6. Get together with some friends and tell a humorous story from your childhood with a moral or lesson you learned.

Epilogue

ON YOUR MARK. GET set. Go! You have all the basic tools now for finding just the right topic, brainstorming, researching, writing and delivering an excellent speech that should hit home with your audience. Use some of these new tools right away and not only will you remember them, but in time they will feel natural. You will start to use many of these skills without even having to think about them.

When you are done with the big speech, or your course on public speaking is completed, stick the book on the shelf but keep it handy. Down the road you are going to have many more opportunities to deliver great speeches. When that time comes, pull the book down from the shelf, blow the dust off the sleeve and refresh you memory, spark some new ideas and put the tools back into practice. Practice makes perfect says the old cliché. There is a lot of wisdom in that saying.

So take a deep breath . . . or two or three, put your new tools into practice and soon you will discover that you are not just a speaker but a great speaker. After all, you have learned how to speak well and you speak easy!

Appendix One
Some Important Terms

Aristotelian Proofs: The ancient Greek philosopher, Aristotle, noted that the most persuasive speeches employed three characteristics: Ethos, Logos and Pathos.

Articulation: Attention focused on pronouncing a series of words in phrases or sentences.

Body of Knowledge: Refers to what we as a society, academy or organization collectively know or understand about certain issues, philosophies or sciences. When we disseminate knowledge, sometimes the body of knowledge increases.

Brainstorming: An early process in the preparation of a speech when the speaker notes as many ideas, issues and concerns relating to his topic as he can.

Cadence: A term that refers to the fall of the voice particularly at the end of a sentence or a phrase.

Communication Apprehension: The common fear of speaking in small or large groups of people. Also called stage fright or speech anxiety.

Dabar: An ancient Hebrew word which roughly translated means "word-event."

Demographics: The study of people and the particular part of an audience they represent. Demographic considerations include age, gender, ethnicity, economic status and group affiliations such as religious background or political persuasion.

Design: The organizational structure of a speech.

Ethics: The science or principles of morality. In speech, unlike etiquette, which is not mandatory, ethics are expected.

Ethos: A speaker's personal character and credibility. Aristotle argued that ethos was an important factor in persuading audiences.

Etiquette: A non-binding code of conduct for social or professional situations. Although not mandatory, a speaker who has good speech etiquette will pay close attention to the customs of his or her audience.

Inflection: The adjustment we make to the pitch of our voice. Inflection moves the pitch up or down.

Informative Speech: Shares information that inspires understanding and empowerment among the members of an audience without having persuasion as its goal.

Logos: The use of logic, reason and verifiable knowledge to persuade an audience. Like ethos and pathos, logos is one of the Aristotelian Proofs and an important tool in persuasive speaking.

Magnification: Aristotle noted that focusing a speech on a particular event, occasion or person tends to intensify or enlarge the experience of it. Not to be confused with "exaggeration."

Manipulation: From the Latin word *manus*, meaning hand. A speaker deploys manipulation by arranging ideas in a devious way in order to trick the audience. To manipulate someone is to handle them or manually arrange ideas. In a colloquial sense, we might say a manipulator "plays" his or her audience by "fixing" knowledge and/or the situation.

Maslow's Hierarchy of Needs: A theory put forth by the twentieth century psychologist, Abraham Maslow, who argued that people are generally motivated by their needs and that fundamental needs must be met before the proposal of secondary needs can be offered. The desire to meet higher needs rests upon the fulfillment of more essential needs. Beginning with our physiological needs, the hierarchy of needs ascends to safety and security, love and belonging, esteem and competence and ultimately arrives at the need for self-actualization.

Monroe's Motivated Sequence: A common and effective design for persuasive speeches developed by former Purdue University scholar, Alan Monroe, in 1935. The five stage motivated sequence is still one of the most effective speech designs today. The stages are capturing attention, demonstrating a need, satisfying a need, visualizing the results, and the call to action. Each stage should be fully and equally developed.

Mythos: The use of myth, folktale, or fable to persuade an audience. Although not one of the Aristotelian Proofs, rhetoricians have noted its powerful effect in the art of persuasion.

Opinion: Idea or perspective founded on non-verifiable information.

Pathos: Eliciting compassion, empathy or other strong emotional feelings from the audience. Pathos is the third component of the Aristotelian Proofs.

Personal Knowledge: Information or understanding based on personal experience.

Persuasion: From the Latin word *suadere*, which means to urge or advise. To persuade is to provide the opportunity and the understanding necessary for an audience to make an informed, wise, and favorable decision concerning the speaker's proposal. The goal of persuasive speaking is to motivate the audience to think differently or to act in a new or specific manner.

Pitch: A musical term, which refers to the rise and fall of a musical tone. When we speak, our voice is our instrument. There ought to be a musicality to our speaking as our voice rises and falls reflecting the mood of our speech.

Plagiarism: A form of stealing; plagiarism is taking the work of another and claiming it as your own. Unethical and illegal.

Point Structure: The arrangement or construction of an individual idea within the overall design of a speech.

Process of Persuasion: The mental and emotional process which your audience needs to experience if it is going to be motivated to change the way they think or act. Each step in the five-step process is dependent on the fulfillment of the prior one. The steps are awareness, understanding, acceptance, retention and enactment.

Pronunciation: Speaking or uttering individual words with attention to correct or common speech.

Refrain System: A sentence, phrase or idea, which is repeated periodically throughout the speech to maintain attention, sustain focus and/or heighten the mood of the speech.

Speakeasy: A speakeasy was an illegal bar or tavern during the prohibition era in America. Access to a speakeasy was granted only when the right word was spoken.

Statement of Purpose: A crystallizing sentence, which tells the audience what the speaker is going to talk about and how the speaker will talk about it.

Summary Statement: Quickly and imaginatively sums up and closes each point.

Stereotyping: Judging an entire group of people based on the impressions formed by the words or actions of individuals within that group.

Transitional Indicators: Brief phrases, statements or individual words, which direct the audience toward the type of supporting evidence or material a speaker is using in a particular supporting point.

Transitional Statement: Introduces each point by creatively announcing to the audience the purpose of the point to follow.

Verifiable Knowledge: Information or understanding of a particular subject, which can be proven, supported, demonstrated and/or confirmed in some way other than our own experience of it.

Appendix Two
For Further Reading

Buttrick, David. *Homiletic: Moves and Structures.* Published by Fortress Press back in 1987, not only did this book become the preaching book of the year, Buttrick's excellent work has influenced an entire generation of preachers. Buttrick takes speakers out of the "three point" speaking mode and challenges them to see speaking in motion. This is a highly recommended book for those who speak in religious settings and those who don't.

Griffin, Cindy L. *Invitation to Public Speaking.* A good textbook published by Thomas and Wadsworth but like other textbooks of this type it will take you some time to work your way through it.

Jaffe, Clella. *Public Speaking: Concepts and Skills for a Diverse Society 4th Edition.* A newer text (2004) published by Thomson and Wadsorth. This resource not only includes a thorough textbook but also makes use of a CD-Rom and on-line support.

Ong, Walter J. *Orality and Literacy: The Technologizing of the Word.* Routledge published this excellent book, which examines the spoken word as we evolve from a literate culture to an oral one. Less about how it is done and more about how it is changing.

Osborn, Michael and Osborn, Suzanne. *Public Speaking, 5th Edition.* Published by Houghton and Mifflin, this is the first text I examined when making the switch from teaching Homiletics (preaching) to public speaking. It is on my suggested reading list for my intro speech students. It is involved but thorough. Like Jaffe's book, it is challenging for intro students to get through the whole text in any depth in one quarter.

Perelman, Chaim. *The Realm of Rhetoric.* Published by Notre Dame Press a few years back (1982) this book is less about the how of speaking as it is about the what. It would be a challenging read for most intro students, but well worth having a look at once you have been speaking for a while.

Perlman, Alan M. *Writing Great Speeches: Professional Techniques You Can Use.* Published by Allyn and Bacon in 1998 as part of the Essence of Public Speaking Series. Perlman, Director of Executive Communications for Kraft Foods, is a seasoned, professional speechwriter.

Simmons, Annette. *The Story Factor: Inspiration, Influence, and Persuasion Through the Art of Story Telling.* A fairly recent book (2001) published by Perseus Publishing. This is an excellent resource particularly if you want to develop your communication skills in business. Simmons demonstrates how story is used as an effective and persuasive tool in a variety of ways and contexts.

INDEX

About Mark Giuliano

Mark Giuliano is a speech professor at the Savannah College of Art and Design, a speechwriter, a public speaking coach, and an ordained minister in the Presbyterian Church (USA). Mark is also a seasoned, international speaker who is regularly invited to speak and offer workshops for a variety of events and conferences throughout North America. For more about Mark, to arrange individual coaching or to book him as your next keynote speaker, please visit www.easyspeech.net.

Printed in the United States
203226BV00002B/49-90/P

9 781878 853851